REA

Helping Chronically Addicted Adolescents

Problems, Perspectives and Strategies For Recovery

Helping Chronically Addicted Adolescents

Problems, Perspectives and Strategies For Recovery

Cardwell C. Nuckols, Ph.D.
A.G. Porcher III
Doug Toft

 Human Services Institute
Bradenton, Florida

TAB Books
Division of McGraw-Hill, Inc.
Blue Ridge Summit, PA 17294-0850

Human Services Institute publishes books on human problems, especially those affecting families and relationships: addiction, stress, alienation, violence, parenting, gender, and health. Experts in psychology, medicine, and the social sciences have gained invaluable new knowledge about prevention and treatment, but there is a need to make this information available to the public. Human Services Institute books help bridge the information gap between experts and people with problems.

FIRST EDITION
FIRST PRINTING

© 1994 by Cardwell C. Nuckols, A.G. Porcher III, and Doug Toft
Published by HSI and TAB Books.
TAB Books is a division of McGraw-Hill, Inc.

Library of Congress Cataloging-in-Publication Data

Nuckols, Cardwell C.
    Helping chronically addicted adolescents / by C.C. Nuckols.
       p.   cm.
    Includes bibliographical references.
    ISBN 0-8306-3768-0 (pbk.)   ISBN 0-8306-3769-9 (hard)
    1. Teenagers—Drug use. 2. Teenagers—Alcohol use. 3. Narcotic addicts—Rehabilitation. 4. Narcotic addicts—Mental health.
5. Alcoholics—Rehabilitation. 6. Alcoholics—Mental health.
I. Title.
    [DNLM: 1. Alcoholism—rehabilitation. 2. Substance Dependence—in adolescence. 3. Substance Dependence—rehabilitation. WM 270
RJ506.D78N73   1992
362.29'0835—dc20
DNLM/DLC
for Library of Congress   92-2305
                                               CIP

Questions regarding the content of this book should be addressed to:

Human Services Institute, Inc.
P.O. Box 14610
Bradenton, FL 34280

Acquisitions Editor: Kimberly Tabor
Development Editor: Lee Marvin Joiner, Ph.D.
Copy Editor: Pat Holliday
Cover Design: Holberg Design, York, Pa.
Cover Photography: Thompson Photography, Baltimore, Md.

Contents

Preface

The Young American Entrepreneurs

One of my consulting trips to Los Angeles brought me to the heart of Watts. Through some friends who were members of Narcotics Anonymous, I'd arranged to meet a young man, a drug dealer. He was fifteen.

I knew I was dealing with no ordinary 15-year-old when I saw him step out of a stretch limousine. This person was too young to have a driver's permit, yet when he emerged from the car I noticed that he sported two handsful of diamond rings. He also had an entourage of bodyguards.

I asked this young man what he did, and he described himself as "an American entrepreneur, doing it the American way." While there was no way I could verify his income from selling drugs, I had little doubt that it exceeded $100,000 per year.

As I listened to him, I realized that any therapist or addictions counselor who would attempt to work with him had to ask one question: We, who offer the hope of recovery and sobriety—what is it we have that this adolescent could possibly want? Furthermore, what does the larger community have that this adolescent wants? I believe that we have much to offer him. But it took no genius to realize that an offer of twenty-eight days in drug treatment and a part-time, minimum-wage job at a fast-food restaurant would fall on less than receptive ears.

Now think about the normal developmental needs of an adolescent. Go back, if you will, to your own adolescence and think about what *you* wanted. I remember a desire for novelty, for excitement, for status among my peers—all paired with a need to test boundaries. I believe this is typical for adolescents.

It's essential for us to realize that the culture of drinking, drugging, and dealing meets those needs. Coming to this realization may be profoundly disheartening. Yet it is reality for thousands of adolescents in America. If any of us are to begin to heal—parents, children, or communities—we must start from this truth.

Indeed, this is the starting point of *Chronically Addicted Adolescents.* As you read, remember that our subject is young adults as much as adolescents. Furthermore, it speaks to a trend that started back in the 1960's, one that was originally called *social breakdown syndrome.* That loose-fitting label pointed to young men and women who failed to pass the familiar developmental milestones of adolescence. Even though they matured physically, their social, emotional, and intellectual developed lagged behind their peers. In the 1960's researchers offered several ideas about why all this happened but no solution was forthcoming. The problem has grown until now we see elementary-school children addicted to crack cocaine and amphetamines.

Earlier in my career as a therapist and consultant to drug treatment programs, I accepted the prevailing wisdom. Usually, our clients were recovering alcoholics and addicts with some prior history of responsible living.

Many of them had married. They had formed families. They had held jobs. And many knew something about solving the basic problems of daily living. This was often true of the most distressed wino who came through the door. Our job was rehabilitation, a term that connotes returning people to a position they once held in life.

Today, when working with adolescents and young adults, I make none of these assumptions. Our task has changed from rehabilitation to *habilitation*—that is, helping clients gain fundamental life skills they have never learned. To state it crudely, often there's little or nothing to rehabilitate. Steering these young people down the path of sobriety is just the beginning of our task. They need vocational guidance and secondary school diplomas (GEDs). Often they need to contend with criminal records, abusive parents, and communities that offer no incentives for recovery. Add to this the fact that years of addiction and immersion in the drug subculture has arrested their mental and emotional development. Becoming a well-functioning adult is tricky enough for an adolescent who is maturing adequately. For a 15- or 16-year-old with the body of an adult and the worldview of an 8-year-old, the task may seem hardly worth attempting. It's often much easier to get stoned.

Chronically Addicted Adolescents is divided into three main sections. In Part I, we offer portraits of adolescents who are addicted. While some identifying information in these accounts has been changed, their essence is unaltered. We offer these portraits in the spirit of Step One of Alcoholics Anonymous: *Admitted that we were powerless over alcohol, and that our lives had become unmanageable.* In other words, recovery begins when we tell the truth about who we are.

As I reread the material in Part I, I am reminded that chronically addicted adolescents often are referred to among treatment professionals as "everybody's failures." Too often these young people represent the school's failures, the family's failures, and the criminal justice system's failures. These portraits of chronically addicted adolescents hit me in the gut, because we've worked with hundreds of them.

Part II offers some perspectives on how this tragedy unfolded. In particular, I focus on three factors: (1) aversive community and family environments; (2) early experience with new drugs; and (3) psychological immaturity. I emphasize the profound effect of newer addictive substances such as *crack* cocaine and *ice*. It's common to find 8-year-olds using crack, experiencing a *hit* that rocks the brain in six to seven seconds—twice as fast as they'd experience a high from sticking a needle in the arm. These kids are experiencing far different effects from even 13- and 14-year-olds who are a more developmentally mature and experimenting with alcohol and low-THC marijuana.

Add the effects of a vicious cycle: poverty, deprivation, loss of family, physical and sexual abuse, and early school failure. Also look at television news reports about drive-by shootings, guns and knives in schools, a bulging criminal justice system and gang-related incidents in our neighborhoods. Bring together these pieces, and you will begin to understand why the last two decades have brought an increase in adolescent suicide rates of almost four hundred percent.

While recognizing all of this, we can still find options for these adolescents. Among all the tales of human wreckage are individual stories of recovery, strength, sobriety, and hope. Through drug treatment programs that take into account the daily realities of addicted adolescents, we can make a difference. By providing healthy surrogate families and role models in the community, we can make a difference. And by creating transitional living environments—*recovery houses*—we can allow these adolescents to resume the task of becoming mature adults who can contribute to society. I have seen it happen. And I offer the strategies in Part III as a way to begin.

Cardwell C. Nuckols
May 1993

Portraits

The official date for the founding of *Alcoholics Anonymous* is June 10, 1935. That was the day when Bill Wilson, an alcoholic stockbroker, met Dr. Bob Smith, an alcoholic physician, in Akron, Ohio. On that day, these men promised to help each other stay sober for the rest of their lives. Today the principles of their personal program for recovery, which later became the Twelve Steps, is a lifeline for millions of addicts around the world.

That chance meeting is 1935 led to a miracle: recovery for thousands of alcoholics and addicts worldwide. And the effects of that miracle, though far-reaching, have not touched the lives of countless addicted adolescents. They live, move, and dream on streets where Bill has not yet met Bob. The following pages narrate some of their stories.

One note: Because crack cocaine and ice are the drugs of choice for many chronically addicted adolescents today, they receive special attention in this book. Please remember that alcohol abuse and addiction is prevalent, and a heroin epidemic looms real on the horizon of the 1990's.

... 1

Profiles
of Addicted Adolescents

ABOUT JACK

Jack's story is told by a counselor who worked with him.

Jack came to us after he got busted for *cannabis*—marijuana. His home detention worker wanted him to come into our facility and get some treatment. Previously Jack had gone to two different camps for commitment. He had been in the criminal justice system since he was thirteen years old; it started with a sexual battery charge against him for allegedly raping a 3-year-old girl.

Jack's mother and his stepfather are both crack cocaine addicts. They live in New York. Grandmother raised Jack, and his brother has been in the system since age thirteen also. From time to time, when they are upset with their grandmother, both boys go to live with their mother. But they don't seem to get in trouble in New York; they only get in trouble here in Texas with the grandmother. The father is very strict, even though he is a crack addict. I can't put those two facts together. Anyway, the boys don't get into any trouble with mother.

When Jack came to our unit he didn't do anything. No goals. He was just here. As far as abiding by rules and regulations, he was a real joker. He has this racial thing about blacks and whites being together that upsets him real bad. He is the person who upset a white boy on the unit by always calling him "Cracker."

We released Jack last Thursday. I talked with his grandmother today during our session, and he was smoking pot again this weekend. This afternoon I called his probation officer and reported it to her, and she is looking at commitment for him. I really don't know what more I could have done with him. I enrolled him in school. He had dropped out of high school; suspended from two, expelled from one.

So I went to this outreach program in his neighborhood and got Jack enrolled. They did a three-day assessment on him to find out where he was at academically so that he could work on his G.E.D. He didn't report this morning.

Jack belongs to a *kid's club*. They sell crack, and they smoke pot, but they are not into alcohol. He only began to use marijuana last year, at age fifteen, so he was late.

His home environment is prostitution, crack cocaine, transients, alcoholics—right near the bus station downtown. They moved there only about eighteen months ago, so this could be another reason for the late usage of dope.

If I were to try and guess Jack's developmental age, in terms of his functioning here and his abilities, I'd place him at age thirteen. About twelve or thirteen. When a person is about twelve or thirteen, what kind of life skills do they really have? I would say beginning skills—beginning to be a teenager or young adolescent. You see it in the way he acts out. He wants attention. One of the other kids here made the comment that Jack just messed around too much. Imagine that—for another teenager to say he was just too silly.

I also think that Jack and his brother were in an apartment complex where not only his mother but the lady upstairs used. They went out looking for crack cocaine and maybe it would be a day before they would come back. Jack was responsible for his younger brothers and sisters —five kids—plus three children who were from upstairs.

And I am sure that Jack has seen a lot of men beat women. That is probably part of the apartment complex life. I didn't feel like I was qualified to get into that, so I kind of asked him about it and then just went on with his therapy.

I felt sad about this, because I couldn't get anywhere with him. He wouldn't let me. He wouldn't let anyone. It's like he was just existing here, just a person who had a bed, another body for the unit head count.

I think he began to listen to me a little bit because I started talking the language he knew. He once mentioned to another counselor here that I was his girlfriend, and I had to straighten him out about that: 'I am your counselor not your girlfriend.' He was beginning to feel real close to me and when I took him for the assessment at the outreach place. 'You are not going to leave me here are you?' he said. 'Yes,' I said, 'I am; all day.'

The first day he was here he did some collage work in the afternoon. The kids were supposed to look through magazines and find pictures of people who represented people in their family. He picked no one.

I think that if you look at the community situations, what we are talking about here is the absence of positive male and female role models, especially for the young male. There is a total absence of positive male factors. Where are they going to learn, how are they going to learn responsibility? The role models are there; it's just that they are overshadowed by the crack dealers and the pimps and the Cadillacs and the drugs and all of the stuff he has been emulating. That is all the input he has, and those are the authority figures he has internalized.

BOBBY'S STORY

This account also comes from a counselor.

Bobby was about twelve or thirteen years old. I had seen him after he had been arrested for robbery. Also, he had been dealing crack cocaine and using marijuana. His mom and dad were in prison. At one point the mom had several boyfriends in and out of the home. Bobby had an older brother who took drugs, and one of his grandmothers dealt drugs as well.

It seemed, though, like the other grandmother was a positive role model for him. Surprisingly, that was the dad's mom, who was involved with church. Meanwhile, the dad was in prison for drug usage, and aunts and uncles were also involved in a lot of drugs. Now there was a real chaotic family—one that did not participate in treatment.

They lived downtown, in a low income neighborhood where there aren't a lot of positive role models—some, but not a lot. Three years ago there used to be more, but now they have moved out and the lower income families are living there. Most are on AFDC and food stamps.

Bobby was in a gang, a group of people who were involved in clan rivalry, the use of drugs, and selling drugs. He talked a lot about wanting to be a professional football player but wasn't doing well in school. A lot of the reason he was selling drugs was so he could buy the kind of shoes that everybody else was wearing and buy the kind of clothes that everybody else was wearing . . . you know, to not be different.

I was working in a private hospital and saw Bobby for about a month. The problem was there was really nowhere to refer him. We could refer him to the county mental health center, but he had transportation problems. I doubt very seriously if he followed up, and I didn't check to see.

There was really no way to deal with all the problems Bobby had. He needed to address substance abuse problems; he needed to address the family problems and get mom in for treatment. We needed to see if we could help her to get off the juice and get her some vocational training, get her a job, get her self-esteem up. There was a lot of chaos all over his extended family within the neighborhood.

The other issue with Bobby was his low self-esteem and chronic depression. It had to do with a death. The way he told the story was that it involved him, a friend, and his friend's brother. They were all at his friend's house and they were playing with a gun. It was Bobby who pulled the trigger; they didn't think a bullet was in there and they ended up killing the brother. Both kids went to jail. That was one of the areas we worked on quite a bit, because he had killed another little kid. A lot of grief work. Yeah, he had to forgive himself for that. We worked a lot on that. We also worked on his language and his spelling.

Bobby wasn't dependent but he abused drugs. His being in with gangs and gang activities—we talked about all that, too. That brought up a lot errors in his thinking about why he was doing it: anger, and false pride. Through it all he was real depressed; felt like he was nothing and everybody knew he was nothing.

I did as much as I could in that short period of time but never did get a chance to work with the family. A lot of what needed to be done was to get some stability in that home. Mom was not accountable. She was drinking and she had all these different men coming in and out, and it seemed as though they were more important than Bobby.

He was allowed to go out on the street—no real limits set for him. He really wanted somebody to be there for him. He was looking for a parent. It was one of those cases where I just felt bad that he was leaving and there was nothing out there for him.

TOMMY'S STORY

Tommy's story appears in his own words from an interview. The interviewer's questions and comments are italicized. At the time of this interview, Tommy was sixteen.

Tommy, I am going to ask you a few questions and I would like you to just be as comfortable as you can. Answer as honestly as you can, okay?

Okay.

Any questions before we get started, anything you want to say?

No.

Okay. We are going to start by asking if you would describe briefly your parents, your mother and father.

First of all, my father I have no relationship with. When I was two years old, my parents got divorced and I haven't seen him, so I really can't describe him.

You have never seen him?

I seen him once but I was under the influence of that stuff they put in your arm for surgery, and so all I seen was a blur.

How old were you then?

About fifteen.

What were you having surgery for?

I was in a gang fight and got busted up.

So he lives nearby?

He lives in the Seattle area, but his wife doesn't care for me too much because of what I am.

What's that?

An alcohol, drug user, and criminal.

Did you have a relationship with him before he got remarried?

No, never had. Last time I seen him I was around five years old, and he had left some stuff in his house . He was moving away and he had left some stuff that he wanted to give to us. He met us at a store and gave us the key and we went to his house and got whatever it was.

You don't have any relationship with him? Do you care?

That is one thing I would like to bring up. This Sunday is visitation. My sister——real sister from the same mom, same dad——got on to my dad because they used to be really close. She kept saying to him, 'Well you need to be with your son more.' She really jumped on his shit. So he called my mom and asked if he could come this Sunday. My mom asked me and she give me until Saturday to decide.

Have you made a decision yet?

I have no idea what I am going to decide. Because if he does come I wouldn't recognize him. If he walked through the door and you asked, 'Is that your dad?' I wouldn't know. And I would feel weird about him coming seeing me now. Two months, three months ago he didn't know if I was dead or alive. So it's like somebody going off to war; you wonder if they are ever coming back. I want to see him because he is my dad. I mean, thanks to him I am here today. But in the sense that he didn't care and left us, that pissed me off.

That kind of hurts.

So it's going to be a big decision. But on the other hand, I've got my mom. Now me and my mom, we don't have a son/mother relationship. It's more like you wash my back and I'll wash yours——more or less best friends.

What do you mean by back washing?

If I help her, she'll help me. If I do her a favor, if I wash her car, she'll let me use it. And I don't have a license. Her knowing I don't have a license—she will still let me use the car. If I vacuumed the house when I was living with her and I came up with fifteen bucks, I'd ask, 'Mom, will you buy me a case of beer?' She would go get it. If I came up with forty dollars, it was, 'Mom will you get me a bag?' 'Give me the money.' That's how it works. I could tell my mom, 'Mom I just got four girls pregnant last night and she would be like, well, that's your own ass. I still love you cause you are making me a grandmother but that's your own ass.'

Do you have any stepdads?

I have had in the past four stepdads. The first one—well, I was kind of young but I still remember, he was an abuser.

What do you mean when you say he was an abuser?

He never abused me or my half-brothers or my sister. But he always abused my mom: slapped her, punched her and threw her around; threw her to the window. We were too young. If he would do it today, he would be a dead man, but I was too young, too small. I couldn't do nothing about it. I let it ride. Finally they got divorced.

How did you feel about it while it was happening?

I was ticked off at that age. You know, at six years old you don't get ticked off very easy. I was pissed, but then I thought, well, that's mom and that's dad; they are just having fun.

Did you feel anything else aside from being pissed?

No, it's weird because I just thought it was normal. They're just playing; they will quit in a little while. And that started me and my brother fighting, fighting, fighting.

Then Mom got married to another guy. He was more or less a drill sergeant. That marriage only lasted four weeks. So you know, they all got married just to get married.

When you say 'more or less a drill sergeant,' what do you mean?

He was like: 'Fold your shirts and put them in your drawers. Make your bed every single day.' He would check the drawers and say, 'What are you doing with play clothes in with school clothes? How many times have we went over and over and over this. You got a B on your paper. You're punished.'

So he asked you to do a lot of things; he had a lot of tasks he wanted you to do.

And that made me mad. I was around the age eight—no about nine or ten—and I was getting to the point, step-dads, they are not my real dad. So I started talking back. I would just leave the house and go down to the pool, go swimming, and go throw my boomerang.

Then my mom met this last guy, Walt. This guy would wake up at four o'clock in the morning every morning, no matter—Monday through Friday, Saturday or Sunday,

Christmas, Halloween, Thanksgiving—four-thirty every morning. He'd drink coffee till 6:00 a.m., and if it was Saturday, drink beer till noon, or whenever he passes out. So, you know how that went.

How did he do?

He had two sons of his own. Both in high school. One was on the football team, so his dad didn't really care. But his other son, Walt, he was sort of like me, a hell-raiser. He didn't care about nothing. Me and Walt hit it off, right off the bat. You couldn't separate us apart. We would get in trouble and both blame each other for the same thing, knowing neither one of us did it. 'Walt did it.' 'No, Tommy did it.' We never fought and we never argued. He had a car and he took me everywhere I wanted to go, and I would get him drugs.

We hit it off, but he moved away. He moved away with his mom, cause Walt's the type person that says: 'If the heat gets too hot, just go over to the next person.' Go over where the grass is greener. His mom is married to a multimillionaire, so he had it made.

I stuck around for two more years, and everything just kept getting worse and worse and worse. This guy, all he would do is drink, and drink, and drink. I remember one time I got a whipping for not putting the bread tie back on the loaf of bread. I was at the age of saying, 'I'll do whatever I want to, screw you.' And my mom would always jump in the way. He was six foot six, and a little woman four-eleven ain't going to stop too much. So he would throw me around and throw my brother around, but I was always the main one. I was always the one to say, 'Screw you.' He would hit me and I would say, 'Screw you.' Then my brother was like, 'Yes sir, yes sir, yes sir.' Then my sister, she was more or less into the cure, witches, and wicker and Ouija boards. She was always in her room with candles and black on. Nobody even noticed Carol.

How often were you spanked?

Well, say it is Monday and I just got on restriction for not doing my chores. Come Thursday I was flicking him off, throwing shit at him. So it was every other day, two or three days a week. And then right towards the end it was every day: 'Fuck you! Fuck you! I don't give a damn what you say.'

He drank every day?

He drank every day.

Did he use other stuff?

He did once that I know of. Marijuana. He was a real country hick, so he didn't do drugs. He was more or less of a drinker. I mean, we used to go to a bar where kids were allowed in but couldn't drink; they could just play pool or video games as long as their parents were there. They were allowed to have cokes, and if they were caught sipping on a beer, then everybody in the party had to leave.

We went up there one night and he was pretty drunk. He was shooting pool with me. It was one of our better nights. He had backed up into this guy and the guy said, 'Oh, excuse me, I'm sorry.' He just turned around and blew up in his face. Hit him with a pool stick, which had the cops there. I had to push him out and put him in the truck and drive off with him in the truck. He picked fights a lot, so he had a real, real bad anger problem . . . real bad.

Was it like yours?

No it didn't take anybody to piss him off, but it takes somebody to piss me off.

Now let me see, that's two of your stepfathers?

Three. Now there's Larry. This last year, my mom started heavily into crack. And around May she had met this guy named Larry.

What was she doing before crack?

Beer, pot and coke every night. She controlled it, it was like once a week, then twice a week, and then every day. And this guy Larry would take fifteen dollars, leave, and come back in two days and have thirty-five hundred—just by buying a fifteen-dollar rock, cutting it up, and selling it, and reselling it, and reselling it.

June eighth I went to jail. I had a grand theft auto charge, so they locked me up. Before I went to jail we had it hard. We would eat beans once a day, I mean canned beans—no milk, no cereal, no nothing—no eggs; not even ketchup was in the refrigerator. Really, really hard times. My mom had lost her Cougar, her brand new ten-thousand-dollar car. She lost a thirteen-hundred-dollar ring that she pawned off for forty dollars. She lost three VCR's, and all of my tapes. I had over three hundred cassette tapes, all pawned off. I had two hundred CD's—pawned them off. That didn't really matter to me, because they were all stolen, but it was the point of the thing: They were mine, so why did you screw with them?

Then Larry shows up and mom got a new car. My brother and my mom said everything just starting pumping in—a brand new car, stereo, brand new everything. Furniture. I didn't see this because I was in jail. I was sitting in there saying, dang you all got all these things, why couldn't you have had them when I was out? Come to find out Larry had like fifteen pending charges. They got married inside the jail.

Who was in jail?

Larry. He is looking now at five to ten years. This guy did anything—petty theft to strong-armed robbery. Invalid use of credit cards. He broke into the chief deputy's house in our county. He really didn't care what happened to him.

So did you meet him?

I met him. He would come over every now and then and say, Hey Tom, how's it going? He was a pretty good size guy. He and mom would go back to the bedroom, and once they went to the bedroom I knew what was going on. So I said, 'Screw you,' and I went down to my girlfriend's house.

What was going on?

They would get high on crack. And to me—I used crack before and I don't want to get back on it. I seen what it did to me.

What did it do?

It put me in a lot of trouble. It put me in jail a lot. And I went from one hundred-sixty pounds down to eighty-five. I mean, I looked like shit. I had longer hair, all stringy; looked like I hadn't washed it about three months. I had the same clothes on. I had a pair of shoes that had nothing but the soles in them. I had to tie a string around them to keep them on my feet.

Then one day I caught myself on the ground looking for more crack and I said: 'Hey wait a minute; what the fuck am I doing?' So I stood up and right then I took my pipe and I threw it against the wall. 'Never again.' It was weird because I quit cold turkey. Then my mom got on to it and I seen slowly but surely what was happening to her: 'Oh, shit here we go again.' My mom lost more than I did. I lost ten percent; my mom lost everything: two cars, three dogs, radios, furniture, food, freezers, and her house. We had just bought a house. We had no money to pay the rent. Boom. The house is gone. We are out on nothing. We barely had the clothes on our back.

Where is your mom now?

She stays with friends. My mom had met this lady through friends of ours. So we moved over with her for awhile. I had just came back from getting out of jail. I went and found out where my mom lived, and it was in the middle of Cracktown. So we lived there for about three weeks. We moved out of there because people were stealing our stuff. Cockroaches in that house could move people. So we got out of there and I went back to jail. I went on the run cause I was supposed to go to court. My mom found a new house with friends, got kicked out of there and now is with another person. So for about a year now it has been friends that have been keeping us going. Slowly but surely we are trying to get a place to stay.

How old were you the first time you used a substance?

I was seven years old and it was marijuana. The very first drug.

How did it progress?

When I was seven my mom handed it to me. We used to have a video camera. About three years ago I was watching me, when I was four or five years old. I was running around saying, 'Give me a toke. Give me a toke, Give me a sip.' So that was really the first time I had took it and felt what it was doing to me.

So they had given it to you before that?

Yeah, but it wasn't really giving it to me; it was like blowing it in my face, putting it with my food. But the first time I took it, it was good, I liked it. Seven years old, going around high. When you are seven you laugh automatically. But when you're high its like that telephone there is funny.

Do you think the use has helped you or hurt you?

In some ways it has helped me and some ways it hurt me. From using I went to dealing, and it has got me money. The bad ways: It has put me in several institutions, put me in jail, put me close to death.

Close to death? How did that happen?

Pretty much gang violence. We were up at the bowling alley one night. It was me and this other guy that was in our gang. We go walking around together. We don't have jackets; it's just a bunch of people running around.

Anyhow, four of us was up at the bowling alley. We was up there shooting pool and we saw part of another gang. These boys think they are so good—the best, the tops—the badest group around. So our goal is to take out. So we were up there, we are shooting pool and I look up and I happen to see one of the leaders of this other gang. I know him. We are good friends. He says, 'Aren't you part of the gang?' I said, 'Yeah. We have our differences but that don't mean we can't still be friends.' He goes, 'Yeah, we can still be friends.'

It was so funny, 'cause he said, 'If we ever get into a shoot out and I shoot towards you I am never shooting at you, I am shooting away from you.' I said, 'Alright I will do the same for you.' So he said, 'Alright, I am just going to let this one slide.' Usually every time you have a confrontation it goes out with guns, knives. There are no rules. He said, 'Alright; we are fixing to cruise anyway. Nice seeing you again.' We used to play football together.

So we walked outside, and here comes more of his guys. So we took off to the left. I had a nine millimeter. I knew the cops were going to be here, so I was going to head towards my house. I had my head down and I ran into a tree. So I fell down, and the next thing I knew, there was that guy that had said, 'Let bygones be bygones.' And there he is with a gun in my face. I said, 'Yo, what are you doing? We were just talking.' He said, 'Yeah, but this is part of the gang: we don't talk.' He stood up and said, 'Turn around.' So he searched me, and I had a big bag of cocaine. He said, 'I will take this for your life.' I said, 'Alright.' I lost my coke but I still got my life. That is just part of gang violence that can get you into trouble.

How do you solve problems when you have problems with other people?

On the average? Guns, knives, weapons. Our motto is, 'Do whatever it takes to survive, no matter what. Take care of number one, yourself.' But now that I'm in here it is hard, because people in here don't know me. If the staff pisses me off, man, I go crazy. I start kicking things around and end up in restraints. But never violence against anybody. Now I never hurt nobody except myself since I been in here. I hurt people on the outside.

So you usually solve problems by use of violence.

Or if it is just a petty problem, I'll just get drunk. I can talk better when I am drunk. It is easier to say things.

How do you feel about yourself?

About myself? I feel good about myself in certain areas. I feel like my mom got divorced all of these times because of us kids. But I feel average. I got my problems, but I always got my strong side. I always look into my strong side.

Say a problem comes up; I stop and I say to myself: 'Well, I got my problems over here, but everybody's got their problems.' I am always a happy person. That's all I love; I love happiness. I hate seeing people cry, and I hate seeing people down in the dumps. If somebody is down in the dumps I'll make a kooky-looking face and I'll start laughing. If the world was like I wanted it, everybody would be laughing all day long. That's the way I feel. I hate pain. I hate sadness because it reminds me too much of my family life. So I just look at the up side of everything.

Have you been in arguments or fights lately?

Yeah, with the staff. Not a fist fight; it was a verbal fight. This week.

Are you doing anything to make this happen?

I do, but I blame it a lot on the pills that they are giving me. They are starting to give me Lithium and some other pills for my anger. I don't really think the pills are doing nothing for me. I think that knowing that I am taking pills is doing stuff for me. I think the pill just goes to my stomach and when I use the bathroom it comes out. But knowing I got a pill in me working, I start to think maybe it's really working. Everything is going my way and it has never done that before. I'm in a spaced-out kind of mode. It's pretty weird. I love it, though. The arguments and all that really haven't been happening the past two days. But up until then it was living hell.

So I feel more responsible. And now that I am here I got a chance to get my life straightened out and get my 'G.E.D.' I don't care what anybody says: A 'G.E.D.' is better than nothing.

But in other ways I see people who are like me. Yeah, they'll knock a sign over. But me, I'd rip it out and stick it in somebody's window. I feel more like the world clown in my little area of friends. Our friends are the world to us, and I am the clown of the world. I am the crazy guy.

I hang around mainly nine people. Out of those nine people, I am the highest—the one who one that has went to jail the most, been to detention the most, got suspended the most, drunk the most, got high the highest. It seems like everybody is looking up to me. But they're only like fifteen, or fourteen. The older people, when I get around them, I switch feelings and attitudes. When I am around people my age I switch attitudes; when I am around toddlers; I switch attitudes there. I make myself fit in with whatever is happening. I can fit in with anything. So that is mainly how my friends and I get along. If they like something, I'll do it just because they like it. If they want to see somebody jump off the roof, I'll climb up and jump off just cause they want to. As long as it ain't thirty-five feet in the air.

You have been in other treatment before, right?

I have been in detention number of times, spent time in the County jail.

What about other treatment?

I have been in other treatment centers. A couple of them was voluntarily, and a couple of them was . . .

Court ordered?

It wasn't really court ordered. The judge would say, 'I am letting you go but I am requesting you go here.' So I would go just to please him. I have never, ever completed a program. I have always been kicked out or my mom's pulled me out. Hopefully this might be the first.

How is this one different from other ones?

This is my last chance. The judge said, 'I am tired of seeing you in here. I mean, I am starting to call you by your first name. This is it. If you screw up now and I am throwing your ass in jail. I am talking the boys' prison.' This guy is serious this time. So if I screw up here, I will be gone for the next two years. From what I have heard about that place and what I have seen about it, I don't want to go.

What did you learn from this experience? Did you learn anything?

This? The hospital or the judge?

The whole experience: the running and getting arrested and going to detention, then the jail—the whole experience.

Well, I'm a screw up. Tommy, you screw up a lot. It also gives me the idea that they want to lock me up, and that ain't going to do nothing but piss me off. But now that I have been off drugs for over a month, I can think clearly. I look back now and think, 'Goddamn have I screwed up. Next year I could have been in the twelfth grade; I could have been on the football team, getting a scholarship to the university.' Drugs and people and these gangs just stopped me. And going to jail stopped me. Everything is like a brick wall. I look around the brick wall and I got to go through twelve more. This one is taking me three months.

Feel like you have got the energy to make it?

I don't know, because it is rough. Because all my family is either in trouble or a drug user. When I leave here, that is where I am going back to. I'm going back to the gang, where everybody is going to be expecting me to go rob a bank or a store.

Is there anything that I didn't ask that you think is important?

The only thing I can say to whoever is listening is this: If they are young like me, they might try to be cool and want to show off and do all this and do all that. One joint ain't gonna hurt and one beer ain't going to hurt. But stop right there. Drop it and go back to school. Do whatever it takes. Stay in school. Stay the hell away from drugs, and stay out of the court system. I don't want to see nobody go up the road I went up. It is rough.

How It Happens

Though many factors contribute to the problems faced by addicted adolescents, we emphasize three. One is the *early onset of alcohol and drug use*. This is especially devastating when we take into account the nature of the new drugs these young people are often using—among them, crack cocaine and a form of amphetamine known as *ice*.

Second, these adolescents *often fail to mature in the social, emotional, and intellectual realms as adequately as they are mature physically*. Many of them are children in adult bodies. Compare a group of chronically-addicted 17-year- olds with another group of 17-year-olds who are sober, doing well in school, and have college aspirations or other plans for what they want to do in life. Chances are you'll see enormous differences between these young people.

A third factor is these young people's *inability or lack of resources to overcome an adverse early environment*. This refers not only to the immediate family environment but to the qualities of the neighborhood and larger community as well.

. . . 2

Early Encounters
with the New Drugs

There has been a drastic change in the onset of alcohol and drug use. To make this clear, perform a short thought experiment.

If you're a male who has used alcohol or other drugs, and if you came to maturity in the America of the 1950's, the following scenario might apply. Think back to the first time you ever used. You probably drank alcohol, and you were probably around fifteen years old. Chances are that crack cocaine or LSD were not available. During that first fling, you may have gone to a nearby park with some of your friends and drank Colt 45 malt liquor because you heard that it contained the most alcohol. You may have abhorred the taste, but you chugged three or four of them as quickly as you could because you wanted to get drunk. Then you may have all sat around and talked about all the women you had been with, as if you had. For the adolescent of just a few decades ago, this was a cutting-edge experience.

Those of us who lived out this scenario found drinking was a way to test boundaries. It was a path to social status, novelty, and excitement. And when we look at the developmental tasks of adolescence, this picture acquires an even bigger context. One of those tasks, after all, is to take some risks. As therapists, we've often asked ourselves this question: Would we rather have a 20-year-old client who drank a little in adolescence and tested some boundaries or a 40-year-old client who never did? As one client put it, "Part of adolescence is finding out and discovering who you are. You want to live through this. You want to survive."

Now fast-forward to the 1990's. During the past twenty years, we have seen an average decrease in the age that high-risk kids start using alcohol or other drugs. This is especially true of kids from dysfunctional homes or aversive environments. In 1970, the average age of first use was around fourteen. This has decreased steadily and inexorably. We are now treating crack addicts at ages eight, nine and ten. This was simply unheard of twenty years ago. Today these ages are becoming the norm for chronically addicted adolescents. In the high risk population of today, the approximate average age of onset for the high risk male is eleven. For the female, it is eleven-and-a-half.

This is the picture that emerges when we consider use of two of the newest drugs: crack cocaine and a form of amphetamine known as *ice*.

THE SUBJECTIVE EXPERIENCE: CRACK AND ICE

Bakalar and Grinspoon (1976) describe the subjective experience of cocaine use as follows:

> . . . *opiates tend to cause a loss of interest in the self that makes mastery of the external environment irrelevant; the feeling is a kind of Nirvana. In contrast, a stimulant like*

cocaine heightens the sensory and emotional brightness and distinctiveness of self against its environmental ground.

Ice addicts call the sensation of smoking the ice pipe *amping*, for the amplifying of euphoria that it causes. In a recent *Newsweek* article (Lerner, 1989), Dr. Joseph Giannasio, Director of Castle Medical Center Alcoholism and Addictions program states "on the front end it doesn't seem so bad. You stay awake, focused on what you are doing. You feel good about yourself. Where it gets scary is at the tail end."

For both ice and crack addicts there is the feeling of increased mental acuity and alertness. It is the reticular formation that is thought to be involved in the regulation of conscious awareness on one hand and sleep on the other. When there is synchronization of neuronal firing, typically a relaxation and sleep response is observed. However, when desynchronization is observed after stimulant use, it is typically a sign of central nervous system arousal. A deleterious effect of crack and ice administration is its disruption of sleep patterns.

Both crack and ice have been reported by users to produce enhancement of perception and sensation. Auditory, visual, tactile and olfactory senses have been reported to be enhanced. Another aspect of heightened awareness is that of increased sexual stimulation. It appears that the *amygdala* is the major dopaminergic center in the brain primarily involved in sexual excitation. So extreme is the effect on this area of the brain that, following freebase administration, the drug appears to replace the sex partner. It is even been described by cocaine I.V. or freebase addicts that spontaneous ejaculation can occur following administration of the drug. This is accomplished without direct genital stimulation.

Other primary drives and reinforcers that are common to the health and perpetuation of species, such as appetite, are superseded by cocaine (Gropetti, Digukio, 1976). The feeding centers located in the lateral hypothalamus are affected by cocaine. Through cocaine's effect on the dopamine system in this area, an anorexia-type syndrome is observed. It is felt that amphetamine acts in a very similar way.

One of the most commonly observed effects noted in stimulant drug users is the tremendous increase in self-confidence and egocentricity that is caused by the drugs. This self-image enhancement can produce a sense of omnipotence and a personality that mimics *Narcissistic Personality Disorder*, as described in the *Diagnostic and Statistical Manual 3rd Edition-Revised* (American Psychiatric Association, 1987). This authoritative guide to psychiatric diagnosis describes Narcissistic Personality Disorder as a pervasive pattern of grandiosity, lack of empathy and hypersensitivity to criticism.

Most clinicians have observed this phenomenon in the crack addict entering a treatment setting. The addict might look at an alcoholic and say "I do a thousand-dollars'-worth of rock a week. What do you do?" This is said condescendingly, as if the cocaine addict were a cut above the alcoholic.

One important characteristic shared by many drugs is their ability to elevate affect and mood. The assessment of addiction liability in humans traditionally involves comparing the subjective effects of a test drug with those produced by a standard prototypical addictive agent. The addictive potential of a drug that offers mood elevation and euphoria has long been recognized. Studies concerning the biological basis of drug addiction have often focused on the actions of drugs on the brain reward centers. In particular, dopamine systems have been implicated in the brain reward system studies.

Cocaine and amphetamine appear to derive their rewarding effect by their actions on the part of the brain called the *ventral tegmental dopamine system*. It appears that both crack and ice cause their stimulant effect by increasing the activity of dopamine in this part of the brain, therefore producing the rewarding effects of the drug. As a matter of fact, crack and ice are so rewarding that a shift in motivational patterns is observed when we compare crack and ice addicts to alcoholics.

In years past, the threat of loss of job or loss of family were the number one and number two motivators that have propelled alcoholics into treatment. With crack and ice addicts, motivational patterns have shifted. Now legal and financial considerations that are the number one and two motivators for getting the crack and ice addict into treatment. The relationship between these drugs and the brain is so strong that it tends to overshadow many important aspects of the individual's existence. The drug has taken on such importance that threat of loss of family and job are not considered as important as getting money immediately to obtain the drug.

Looking at the love affair between crack/ice and the addict's brain in another way, we can see the ultimate severance of bonding. It appears that these drugs create such a passion within the addict's brain that the mother-child bond is often disrupted. Crack and ice addiction has been implicated in cases where mothers have sold their children in return for small amounts of the drug. They have allowed drug dealers to repeatedly rape their young children in exchange for the drug.

FOUR STAGES OF COCAINE INTOXICATION

According to Siegel (1987), cocaine smokers progress rapidly through four stages of intoxication, although the pace of this progression is based upon many factors.

Euphoria

Stage One is marked by mood sweeps and euphoria. The user is hypervigilant and cannot eat or sleep.

Dysphoria

Stage Two is characterized by the negative feelings of apathy and sadness, along with difficulty in attention and concentration. There is continued existence of anorexia and insomnia.

Paranoia

Stage Three manifests irrational fears of persecution or feelings of extreme jealousy. These may cause the individual to act out, sometime violently.

Psychosis

Psychosis is marked by paranoid ideation and hallucinations. There is a loss of contact with reality, disorientation and loss of impulse control.

Generally, the toxic syndrome from ice will follow the same progression as that of crack cocaine. Still, there is a significant difference between the toxicity observed in the ice addict and that observed in the crack addict and it can be attributed to two things.

The first and most important is the longer half-life of ice. Based upon the alkalinity of body fluids, the half-life of ice can be anywhere from eight hours to thirty-three hours.

Secondly, clinical staff will observe a remarkable elongation of the toxic syndrome. Therefore, with the crack addict, we would observe an easing of toxicity symptoms within hours after discontinuation of use. But it has been observed clinically, in the ice addict, that extreme toxicity can last for days, even up to a week. This has major implications for the design of clinical treatment programs for these addictions.

SECONDARY EFFECTS

Toxic effects of psychomotor stimulant overdose can cause death from respiratory arrest, systemic infectious processes, cardiovascular shock, seizures, hyperpyrexia, cardiac arrhythmias, and cerebral hemorrhage. However, drug overdose is not the only concern with psychomotor stimulant use. The leading cause of death secondary to the taking or administration of crack or ice are: homicide, suicide, and accidents.

Riding the Roller Coaster

As the stimulant addict consumes larger quantities of the drug, the natural self-preservation mechanism is activated. This has been described as the "fight or flight syndrome." The fight or flight syndrome is the body's protective mechanism that allows it to be hypervigilant to its environment. Accompanying this is behavior appearing like paranoia. An individual who is in a dangerous situation should be highly suspicious of his or her environment. With crack and ice we see these natural and normal protective mechanisms gone wild.

Imagine a ride on a roller coaster. Remember that first hill that is so high? You are at the bottom of that hill, seated in the roller coaster. The roller coaster starts to move and it creeps forward ever so slowly. You start to hear the click, click, click of the chain as the roller coaster goes up that first steep hill. You begin to reach the top and when you get there, there is a pause just before you go over the other side. What you feel now is the experience of the adrenalin rush, the experience of exhilaration, the experience of fear—all are a part of the fight or flight syndrome.

These are the exact mechanisms that crack and ice trigger. If you could imagine the roller coaster situation but consider the fact that the drug, through the dopamine systems and via other mechanisms , produces a profound euphoria, you have in many ways the low dose experience of crack and ice.

Delusions

As the dose of crack and ice increases, depression and malaise grows, a dysphoric reaction. As chronic use of these drugs increases, an individual goes from hours to days without food and sleep disruption becomes common. Paranoid delusions can begin to appear.

Paranoid delusions are directly related to some of the violent activity observed in the culture of crack and ice. There are three types of paranoid delusions that can be observed in the stimulant addict:

- **Persecutory Paranoid Delusion**: The addict may be quite toxic and run out of crack or ice. The individual may go out to cop the drug and suspect that someone who may be selling him the drug is out to get him. Over a very small amount of crack, ice or money, someone could get shot or killed. A persecutory delusion involves the individual having an unrealistic awareness that someone else is out to do him wrong. This is often described in newsprint as the "drug deal gone bad."

- **Jealous Paranoid Delusion**: The crack and ice addict can experience a delusion that often is anchored in interpersonal relationships. This type of delusion involves one partner accusing the other partner, often falsely, of being involved sexually or emotionally with a third party. This can lead to homicide or brutal beatings. Domestic violence can be a by-product of drug-induced jealousy.

- **Erotomanic Paranoid Delusion**: *Erotomania* involves projection of one's thoughts and feelings into another. The erotomanic patient becomes convinced that she or he is passionately loved by another person. In situations where erotomanic paranoid delusions exist, the potential for rape is a very real possibility.

The ice and crack user may experience peculiar delusions of *parasitosis* and sensations of insects under the skin (formication). This may lead to excoriation of the skin. Addicts have been clinically observed to cut into or probe their skin with needles in search of parasites of "cocaine bugs." Also observed in stimulant addicts is a type of visual hallucination often referred to as "snow lights." "Snow lights" are flicks of silver or white light in the peripheral visual field that can even take the form of snow flakes and at times can pervade the entire visual field. The causative factor appears to be constriction of the blood flow to the optic nerve.

Of great concern with cocaine toxicity is its unpredictability. Although one might expect an increased tolerance, a most dramatic effect is a form of reverse tolerance described as "kindling." Kindling involves the increased effect of the drug, especially in regard to seizure and psychotic episodes after repeated administration of the same or lower dose of the drug.

It appears that many of the biological changes associated with stimulant abuse and dependence mimic those associated with stress. Both crack and ice cause an alerting, sympathetic, predominately *catecholaminergic* action. By studying acute and chronic stress models, one can understand many of the acute and chronic changes in levels of neurotransmitters. Generally speaking, acute stress tends to cause an increase in *catecholamines*. A longer or more chronic type of stress tends to deplete the catecholamines. This pattern seems to be observed in both cocaine and amphetamine addicts. Acute administration of crack cocaine and ice increase levels of norepinephrine and dopamine. Chronic administration of the mood altering drugs reduce norepinephrine and dopamine stores and availability at the synapse.

ADDICTIVE POTENTIAL

There are many features that determine addiction potential. Until recently, cocaine addiction was not even considered a drug leading to a substance use disorder. It was only considered a drug of abuse. This alone would lead one to believe there was great psychological potential for addiction but very little physiological addiction potential. With the advent of the American Medical Association's definition of addictive disorder, we see crack and ice as drugs with tremendous addiction potential. The new addiction definition involves (1) loss of control; (2) compulsive use; and (3) continued use despite adverse consequences. As we look at crack and ice we will see that use of either drug can produce extreme dependence.

The way in which a drug is taken into the body is an important variable in determining the likelihood that it will lead to dependence or abuse. Typically, dependence follows when the method of administration is extremely efficient and provides a rapid means of getting the substance into the system. Substances such as crack and ice are rapidly administered and hit the central nervous system in six to seven seconds. Therefore, the likelihood of an instant positive relationship leading to a very early marriage or dependence is probable.

Crack and ice also are drugs that are consistent with episodic use. During these episodes, drug use is compressed into time periods called *binges*, where the individual stays continuously high. These binges are often followed by one or more days of abstinence. This binge pattern, correlated with a rapid addiction, tends to occur when the substance is smoked or taken intravenously. Such is the case with crack and ice.

The half-life of a substance also is a very important variable in determining the potential for substance abuse disorder. Short acting psychoactive substances, such as crack, tend to be more commonly used than substances with longer duration but similar psychoactivity. However, ice is an exception. It has a long half-life, yet enormous abuse and addiction potential.

The whole concept of dependence has taken on various meanings to addiction professionals. In the past, we were attentive to a physical or pharmacological dependence with the hallmark features of drug tolerance and withdrawal. Although it is impossible to separate the mind from the body, there is an aspect of dependence that seems to be extremely important in the area of crack and ice addiction. This is termed "psychological dependence."

Although the term "psychological dependence" can have many meanings, it can be clearly understood as relying upon a drug as a major means of coping. Deprived of the substance—in this case crack or ice—a person is at loss for how to cope with the stressors of their situation or how to escape from the discomfort of their problem. Their psychological dependence is the basis for the observation that *for these addicts drug are not seen as a problem, a solution*.

CHANGING PATTERNS OF ADDICTION

There is a changing scene in our communities today and crack and ice addiction is but a symptom of these changes. In many communities crack is so prevalent that it might be considered a *gateway drug* along with alcohol, marijuana and nicotine. The population boundaries of the crack and ice addict have changed, and users have become younger. It is now common to see crack and ice addicts eight, nine, ten, eleven and twelve years of age.

The problems brought about by this type of addict is a problem that is becoming a festering sore in our treatment system. It is not like it used to be. We do not see

drugs such as alcohol—that cause the long-term chronicity
—and a thirty-year history of use where a person tends to
lose relationships, responsibility and respect. We do not
see nearly as many overdoses as we saw in the heroin
cultures of the sixties and early seventies. With crack and
ice, we see a rapidly progressing illness. It is starting very
early in life. It is creating a multiplicity of problems that
require a plethora or answers. The combination of
creativity and taking the best of mental health and
alcoholism and drug treatment will be critical in meeting
the needs of this population. There is a need for vocational rehabilitation. There is a drastic need for that population attaining high school educations or graduate equiva-
lent degrees (GED).

Something has happened during the decade of the
eighties. The 800-Cocaine telephone hotline (Gold, 1984)
described the cocaine addict of 1983 as a college-educated
(50%), intranasal (61%) user, with a low unemployment
rate (16%) who often earned over $25,000 per year. By
1988, this profile had shifted drastically. The new crack
addict is poorer, less educated, urban and more likely to
be unemployed. The new cocaine or crack addicts have
less support, fewer financial resources and less accessibility
to treatment and self-help groups.

The crack and ice addict is a symptom of a changing
scene out on the streets. We are seeing a younger population that is achieving higher degrees of chronicity at a very
young age. Combining the tremendous craving potential of
crack and ice with the dynamics of relapse found in this
population, we have a formula for difficulty. If we took,
for example, an individual who lived in an area where
there was crack cocaine or ice available, and we added
some dimensions in the environment, such as the scarcity
of self-help, there exists a problem. If we also add the fact

that the individual's family may have some degree of dysfunction, then we start to see the problem mushroom.

Smokeable Stimulants—A Marketing Phenomenon

Another way to understand smokeable stimulants, such as crack cocaine and ice, is to view them as highly effective marketing gimmicks. After all, if you wanted to market a product to an adolescent, you would want it to appear inexpensive. You'd also want it to be highly addictive, a product that satisfies many people and builds a stable group of repeat customers. Crack and ice satisfy these criteria perfectly.

Ice, especially, represents a marketing breakthrough. Crack and ice work with the same neurotransmitters in the brain. But crack's peak effect lasts only for five to seven minutes, while a hit off the ice pipe may last for six to eight hours. In short, a crack high lasts for minutes; an ice high, for hours. Ice is ideal for students who want a high that remains throughout the school day. And for those working eight-hour days, ice is also ideal: You can hit the pipe first thing in the morning, before work, and again at lunch for a quick pick-up. In addition, ice is more "user friendly" than crack since often it is inhaled from a smaller pipe and requires less apparatus than crack.

Both crack and ice have the added advantage of being smokeable stimulants, as opposed to drugs that are injected. Smoking means almost instant gratification, because the drug registers in the brain within six to seven seconds. To achieve the same effect by injecting the drug would take twice as long. What's more, smokeable drugs have much broader appeal than injectable drugs requiring needles to administer: Many middle-class users express an aversion to needles.

Finally, consider the wide availability of amphetamines that can be made into ice. If we were ever to achieve the improbable goal of eliminating cocaine from this country, we would still have an ideal market for ice and other forms of methamphetamine. In fact, a skilled dealer or user can make ice out of legally available chemicals, such as the decongestant Sudafed.

The New Face of Marijuana

Though we've focused in this chapter on crack and ice, we cannot leave out another one of the "new" drugs: marijuana.

The marijuana of the 1990's is a far cry from the drug that older users remember from the 1960's, even though it still enjoys the image of a "soft drug." But when we examine it molecule for molecule, marijuana is about one thousand times stronger than alcohol. It is a very potent drug. Remember that the marijuana smoked back in the 1960's and early 1970's—unless it was *Thai Stick* or some other exceptionally potent marijuana—was less than four percent THC, the drug's psychoactive ingredient. Much of the marijuana available on the streets today consists of eight to twelve percent THC. Some current marijuana has nearly the potency of hashish. We can justifiably say that marijuana is a drug of addiction. And as such a powerful drug, marijuana intoxication impairs performance, both at school and on the job.

Marijuana represents one of our great problems in treating addiction. Among people in recovery, as many as fifty percent of the relapses to alcohol or crack use begin with the smoking of marijuana.

Loss of Connectedness

In ending this chapter we want to offer some personal, subjective reflections on the larger issues behind the use of the new drugs.

It was the psychoanalyst Carl Jung who spoke of our thirst for alcohol as being akin to our thirst for psychological wholeness. To this idea we can comfortably add the words of one recovering addict who said, "There are a lot of people in this world walking around with holes in the middle of their souls." For these people, drugs are Band-Aids for psychosocial injuries, fleeting paths to euphoria. At the same time, these drugs lie. They deliver the illusion of power and control, but then they take it all away.

We believe that crack and ice owe much of their appeal to the loss of connectedness in our society. In many ways, addiction to these drugs is the logical consequence of viewing material goods as more important than spiritual goods. The materialistic view is summarized perfectly by the bumper sticker that says "He who gets the most toys before he dies, wins." This is a slogan for our era, and for the people who believe we are only as good as what we have. Meeting people for the first time, most of us are prepared for the usual questions about educational status, about what kind of money we make, where we live, what schools we attended, and where we work. Seldom do people ask about our qualities as spouses, about our civic lives, or about our church attendance or spiritual perspectives.

Perhaps the most fundamental reason we use drugs— even more fundamental than genetic predisposition or dysfunctional families—is that something essential is missing in our lives. That something may well be connectedness, a vital link not only to what Alcoholics Anonymous terms a "Higher Power," but to the people in our neighborhoods, our voting precincts, and our cities. And the people who stand to lose the most from this development could well be the at-risk adolescents.

... 3

Arrested Development
Children in Adult Bodies

One theme of this book is that the average age when young people start using drugs, often called the *age of onset*, has decreased markedly. The age of onset used to be about fourteen. Today we are seeing children ages ten and eleven using toxic, rapidly addicting substances. Parents and other concerned adults often see the obvious and devastating consequences that flow from this fact. Yet they may overlook three of the major costs to young users: delayed social, emotional, and cognitive development.

The underlying question is this: What happens to childrens' personalities when their lives start to center on the drug subculture at age eleven, twelve or thirteen? In many cases, personality development grinds to a halt. Often these adolescents remain frozen in childhood.

Keep in mind that, beyond early childhood, there are two crucial developmental periods in life: ages eleven through thirteen and ages seventeen through nineteen. Any trauma or disruptions during these periods can have lifelong consequences. These are the years when a child goes from childhood to adolescence, and from adolescence to adulthood. They are periods of tremendous change and vulnerability.

During the age eleven to thirteen period, one of the child's primary tasks is socialization. This is a prime time for boyfriends, girlfriends, and best friends, a "classroom" for honing the social skills that pave the way for satisfying adult relationships. A child who is stoned throughout these years is simply derailed, developmentally speaking. And later, if these addicted adolescents do receive the opportunity to enter drug treatment, they find themselves without the interpersonal skills that cement a lifelong recovery. Giving these adolescents assignments that require them to work with others—tasks as simple as cleaning the kitchen—is like asking them to move to a foreign country without speaking the language. They just have few, if any, of the social, intellectual, or emotional tools needed to do these things.

Even to say that these children stop developing in these three crucial ways—intellectual, social, and emotional—may be painting too rosy a picture. In some cases, their personality development not only stops but regresses. The 15-year-old crack addict may not just be frozen intellectually or emotionally at age twelve; he may actually display the world view and behavior of an 8- or 9-year-old. "You see it even in the young adult addicts, eighteen or twenty years old who come for treatment," says one therapist. "They may be strong as heck, tremendously athletic, and handsome, but when you start to work with them, your first thought is, God, they're so childish. They just don't seem to get with the program. I wish we could turn the pages, but they're stuck back there someplace in the world of an 11- or 12-year-old."

DEVELOPMENTAL PROBLEMS

The following chart is a rough guide to the major tasks children face as they progress through the rites of passage leading to adulthood.

NORMAL MATURATION TRENDS
THE ADOLESCENT PERIOD

From Childhood (6-12 years) →	To Adulthood (over 18 years)
Social	*Social*
Intolerance of others	Tolerance of others
Imitation of peers	Interdependent
Center of the universe	Understands relatedness to others
Emotional	*Emotional*
Feelings of uncertainty	Self-acceptance and adequacy
Anger, lack of empathy	Tolerance and empathy
Cognitive	*Cognitive*
Concrete thinking	Formalized thinking
Everything is either right or wrong	Can abstract, conceptualize, and problem-solve

In the following pages, we explore some of the specific developmental tasks that chronically addicted adolescents often fail to undertake.

Cognitive Immaturity

"All-or-nothing" thinking is prevalent. Ask treatment counselors who work with chronically addicted adolescents about their clients' intellectual development. Chances are you'll get an answer such as this: "Everything is like a final answer to these kids. The world is either all right or all wrong. There are no grey areas. Detailed, thoughtful explanations tend not to work very well. They just want it yes or no, true or false."

This tendency to view the world in rigid, extreme terms is called dichotomous, or "all-or-nothing," thinking. Despite its drawbacks, this lack of intellectual range serves an important function: It reduces anxiety. It reduces the world to simpler categories. Moreover, all-or-nothing thinking allows any of us to avoid confronting a potentially painful truth about ourselves: that we have behavior potentials ranging from good to evil and constructive to destructive.

Bringing this truth to mind calls not only for some measure of emotional stability, but for higher-order thinking skills. Confronting ambiguity, both in ourselves and in the world, is an advanced intellectual skill and a hallmark of a fully functioning adult. Embedded in this skill are the abilities to conceptualize, abstract, consider alternate viewpoints, and live with contradiction and paradox.

While classifying these skills as cognitive, we realize that they are essential to social and emotional development as well. Resolving conflict, solving problems, sustaining relationships—each of these calls on us to transcend all-or-nothing thinking.

Splitting: It's like two different people. Once consequence of all or nothing thinking is especially important to parents and treatment professionals who work with chronically addicted adolescents. When relating to these young people, it's essential to realize that we can be everything and nothing to these young people . . . both at once. An adolescent who loves us at one moment can despise us ten minutes later.

Moreover, an adolescent can seem like two different people with two different staff members. This has profound consequences for us when we use many of the traditional tools for modifying behavior, including behavior contracts. The therapist who has completed a gratifying therapy session with an adolescent may want to extend contract privileges. Nurses, aides, and other members of the treatment staff might react to such developments with surprise, even resistance. One way to reduce tension among the staff is to be sure everyone recognizes the amorphous and highly variable personality of the addicted adolescent. These young people are highly reactive and ready to take not only thinking, but behavior, to extremes. Chronically addicted adolescents can display remarkably different behaviors and thought pattern under different circumstances.

This is sometimes a strategy, adopting different faces for different people to reduce anxiety and erect defenses against the world. An apt name for this phenomenon is *splitting*. The term is significant not only in describing what happens to the addicted adolescent but to any team of professionals working with this adolescent. This clinical challenge may be the ultimate test of staff cohesion.

Concrete thinking is the norm. A key cognitive task for the 11- to 13-year-old is to move from concrete thinking to formal thinking. We use this term in pointing to several skills: the abilities to generalize and abstract, to grasp key principles underlying discrete events, and to see long-term consequences of a behavior.

We usually think of these skills as being essential to success in school. Yet they are also key to successful recovery from addiction. Young people who fail to see how their words and actions impact other people can completely miss the potential benefits of group therapy. They can fail to empathize with others and adopt the powerfully healing perspectives reflected in the following statements: *I'm not the only person who's ever had this problem. Other people are in the same boat, and we can help each other. The people I've hurt deserve amends. We're all in this together.*

Take, for example, the young drug dealer in treatment. His therapist asks him to consider all the people who have died from consuming the product he sells. A typical response from the adolescent is this: "I can't help what happens to those people. Taking the drugs was their choice, their responsibility. And if they hadn't bought the drugs from me, they would have bought them from somebody else." It's essential to realize that such statements can reflect not only an *unwillingness* to empathize but an *inability* to do so. In such cases, any lectures about the toxic or fatal effects can easily amount to wasted breath.

When responding to such a worldview, we often can profit by bringing the consequences closer to home, much as we would with a younger child. Instead of asking an addicted adolescent to contemplate the long-term effects of using drugs on an anonymous customer, we can ask, *What if someone sold some heroin to your sister and she died from an overdose the first time she used it?* The aim here is to make your point as concrete and close-to-home as possible.

Decision-making and problem-solving skills are lacking. It's easy for treatment professionals—even those with years of experience working with adults—to take it for granted that addicted adolescents know how to make decisions and solve problems. Few of us would ask 9- or 10-year-old children to make the kind of major life decisions that often are required of persons being treated for addictions. Yet we can easily find ourselves doing this when working with a 16-year-old crack addict who has been using the drug for six years. Probably this client has had few, if any, opportunities to learn problem-solving skills, especially during months or years of a cocaine-induced fog. It's likely that this young person will adopt an immature problem-solving strategy: *I'll do whatever it takes to reduce anxiety right now and worry about the consequences later.* As one adolescent put it, "You either run from trouble or you get loaded."

Contrast this attitude with the intellectual skills required to solve a problem: (1) defining the problem, (2) generating alternative solutions, (3) listing the possible benefits and costs of each solutions, (4) implementing a solution, and (5) evaluating the outcome. Chronically addicted adolescents from aversive homes and communities usually react instead of responding thoughtfully. Consequently they show intellectual deficits and a poor repertoire of problem solving skills both in school and in treatment for their addictions.

The first problem-solving techniques we learn as infants and toddlers are crying or throwing a tantrum. These are the responses of anger and frustration. Chronically addicted adolescents still may be relying on these two strategies to get their needs met, augmented by a third: using alcohol or other drugs.

Emotional Immaturity

Uncertain emotions and lack of empathy. In the last several pages we've explored the dimensions of cognitive immaturity we may encounter in chronically addicted adolescents. Equally important is a second type of immaturity: emotional immaturity.

One therapist who specializes in working with chronically addicted adolescents expresses it this way:

> *These kids are uncertain about themselves. They're going to vacillate all over the place on us. They lack empathy, and they tend to respond to things by getting pissed off. Refinement of moods is a concept that just doesn't apply to them. The same is true for sentimentality. Things that are more maudlin are definitely not going to be a part of their experience.*

Young people who become dealers often insist on their moral neutrality: They are only offering a product for sale, and the responsibility for any ill consequences that befall their customers belongs solely to the customers. In the words of one adolescent: "If someone wants to buy crack from me, it's their choice. I'm just there to offer it to them. If they choose to use it and end up dead, I don't care." This is tantamount to saying, "If I carry a loaded revolver and accidentally shoot a few people, it's their fault. They shouldn't have been in the way." There's a bumper sticker that sums up this attitude perfectly: "If you don't like my driving, get off the sidewalk."

Low frustration tolerance. A second aspect of emotional immaturity is an inability to tolerate frustration. This is characteristic of the child aged six to twelve who screams,

"I want it, and I want it now!" In contrast, a hallmark of a mature adult is the ability to delay gratification, to sacrifice now for the sake of future gain, and to collect the reward for a task *after* the task has been completed. These qualities are often lacking in chronically addicted adolescents.

Erecting defenses. To cope with the raw facts of addiction, aversive family environments, arrests, or gang violence, many addicted adolescents erect a solid wall of defense mechanisms. One defense, which is well known to professionals in addiction treatment, is denial. We can well say that this defense prevents many of these adolescents from ever "getting with the program." In order to maintain the illusion of competent control over their lives, these young people simply ignore the observable realities. In essence, they say to themselves: "I'm still okay, even though I have a criminal record, have been kicked out of school, and I'm locked in combat with my parents. No one understands. Drugs are great for me, because they keep me alive. Drugs help me be a winner."

Defenses can take other forms. One is rationalization: "If the cops hadn't caught me, I wouldn't be in this mess now." Projection, a defense mechanism that shifts blame to others, was at work in the adolescent who told us this: "If you guys were really sharp, you would tell all the bankers in town not to cash my bad checks. Then I wouldn't have had enough money to buy all this cocaine." Other varieties of these defenses are reflected in these comments: "I got into trouble with drugs because of where I live. Everyone at school does it. My parents do it, so it's okay."

All these sentiments have one thing in common: They create the illusion that we are without choices and live out our lives as the passive victims of external circumstances. Adolescents armed with this view of the world can not only be developmentally arrested but well defended against the possibility of change.

Stuck between dependence and autonomy. Even for children who are maturing adequately, adolescence is a time of contradictions. These are years when we are stuck between dependence and autonomy, between childhood and adulthood. We are expected to act like adults, even as we're required to raise our hands before we go to the bathroom.

Because drug use freezes child development, chronically addicted adolescents are inexorably drawn back to the strategies of childhood. As obvious as this idea sounds—regardless of how times as we read or hear it—it is easy to forget when talking to a six-foot, 19-year-old crack addict. Judging by their physical maturity alone, we'd normally assume that such young people are poised to take on the challenges of adulthood: becoming husbands, wives, citizens, and productive workers. Yet we simply cannot assume this about adolescents who have been steeped in the status, novelty, and excitement of the drug subculture for a third of their lives.

Disruptive behavior and the fear of intimacy. Their defenses and their inability to empathize often leave chronically addicted adolescents isolated. Their lives are often empty of true intimacy or friendship, and they have no clear idea of how to sustain a caring relationship. Consequently, they may retreat into themselves or act out when faced with a central task of recovery: developing relationships not based on using or dealing. One treatment counselor described it this way:

If they start seeing anything that looks like intimacy in a relationship, it scares the hell out of them and so they blow up or disrupt the group sessions. They will pass a note, they will fall out in the floor, they will make an inappropriate gesture, they will get up and walk out.

Social Immaturity

Kids who lack limits. One source of the problems we have been discussing in this chapter is lack of parenting—more specifically, the lack of effective limits in these young peoples' lives. This thought brings to mind the comments of a judge of our acquaintance, one who sat on a committee to draft drug-prevention policies in his state. He recalled that as a 15-year-old he came home drunk on one occasion and angrily insulted his mother. Though he failed to remember exactly what he said to his mother or how she reacted, he graphically recounted his father's response:

"My dad collared me, pushed me up against the refrigerator, and said, 'If you ever say anything like that to my wife again, I will knock your head in. And on top of that you don't come in this house drunk. Now get on the porch, because that's where you're sleeping tonight.'"

We may disagree with the implied violence of this father's reaction, but there's little doubt that he conveyed a clear limit for his son's behavior.

Today we seldom hear of parents setting such forceful standards for behavior. Vast numbers of people in our society have lost the idea that there are simply some things that young people may *never* do without suffering catastrophic consequences.

Profound shifts in family demographics make it harder for effective limit-setting to take place. One of them is the rise in single-parent families, especially where the adult not only works full-time but takes on child-rearing unassisted. These people may be too stressed to parent effectively. And when these parents are addicted or abused themselves, their situation rapidly becomes more desperate. Children of crack cocaine addicts may, for all practical purposes, find themselves *without* parents.

While the lack of limits is a factor that plagues some chronically addicted adolescents, parental permissiveness negatively affects others. Sometimes extreme permissiveness is seen among parents who themselves were abused, or have abused children. Some of them fear being put on the human services "blacklist" and losing their children. So in the name of avoiding the appearance of abuse, or of giving their children the "love" they themselves never had, they let their children function without limits. This gives children tacit permission to experiment with drugs.

Kids who don't know how to socialize. Another aspect of the immaturity we see in chronically addicted adolescents is their inability so socialize, that is, to form relationships and do constructive, friendship-building activities with their peers. Instead, they are frequently steeped in the ethos of the drug subculture: survive, get by, and stay high. Yet when we take these adolescents into a treatment program, we ask them to bond with their peers, disclose their emotions in group and individual therapy settings, and find recreational activities that do not center on drugs. This is like asking a person in a wheelchair to leap over a tall building. If we want to give these young people the experience and hope of recovery, it means providing compensatory experiences for children who lack "social skills."

The culture of narcissism. Narcissus was a mythical young man so in love with himself that he refused all other offers. The goddess Artemis punished him by causing him to fall in love with his own reflection. Ultimately tormented by his inability to embrace himself, Narcissus committed suicide.

Narcissism is an apt word to describe the worldview typically present presented by chronically addicted adolescents. Central to this worldview is the fundamental self-centeredness that addiction promotes. Again, the drug subculture is founded on the premise of taking care of "number one"—doing whatever it takes, legal or illegal, to protect yourself and your drug supply.

Besides, the psychological effects of stimulant drugs such as crack and ice promote narcissism. Often these young addicts display a destructive vanity and self-absorption. Beneath the veil of inflated accomplishment, illusions of grandeur, wealth, power, beauty, and perfect love is often a concealed feeling of inferiority, emptiness, and shame. Beneath the veil of control, however, the narcissistic individual is often afflicted by envy, anger, boredom, and an extreme vulnerability to humiliation.

The seeds for this outlook on life were planted during the generation of these adolescent's parents: the 1960's. During that decade we heard the clarion calls of narcissism: *Tune in, turn on, and drop out. Kill your parents. Do your own thing. If it feels good do it; if it doesn't, lose it.* In the words of one psychologist who came of age in the 1960's:

> *During that time we were given full permission to have 'open' marriages and expected to have a stable of fulfilling relationships. Psychologists made great bucks on that. I mean, my God, how do you have one good*

relationship? That's hard enough. And then they tell us it's normal to have two or three, even though it's possible that no one can do that really well. So people were literally screwing up all over the place.

Since that time, narcissism has become an established diagnosis. And we see its toll in the loss of family connectedness and soaring divorce rates. Missing from this view of life was the notion of taking responsibility, delaying gratification, or working for constructive change. When these perspectives are missing from child-rearing, we sow the seeds of the drug subculture for our adolescents.

Rebels, loners, and pessimists. One set of characteristics cuts across substance abusers, no matter whether their age or addiction. In treatment we find that clients fall into three rough categories: *loners, rebels,* and *pessimists.*

Given what adolescents face out on the streets, it makes sense that they adopt these extreme orientations to life. On the streets, survival means that no one can be trusted. Getting too close to someone invites exploitation. Asking for help or admitting weakness means getting had.

Keeping this in mind, we can hardly be surprised that these people find it difficult to "fit in" on the treatment unit. They hesitate to form relationships. They fail, in the language of Alcoholics Anonymous, to share their stories of "experience, strength, and hope." If successful recovery from addiction means ultimately bonding to a therapeutic community, then these adolescents have little chance of success.

Responding to this means providing something these young people never had: a person who models effective bonding with other people. This is the wisdom displayed in the AA tradition of pairing a recovering addict with a sponsor—another recovering person with a history of sustained sobriety. We, too, can provide sponsors or "buddies" for adolescents who enter the treatment community. In any case, we simply cannot assume that addicted young people will take such a step on their own.

Each of the brands of immaturity described in this chapter—cognitive, emotional, and social—are multidimensional, and their causes are equally complex. As we have seen, they include early drug use and developmental arrest. Equally important is the role of aversive environments, the subject of the next chapter.

Aversive Environments

Chronically addicted adolescents come from diverse backgrounds, sometimes appearing to have little or nothing in common. Yet among these adolescents we frequently find a hidden common denominator: an aversive environment in early life. We see childhoods scarred by emotional, physical, and sexual abuse, as well as a family history of chemical dependency. Exploring how these young people cope with such environments is our purpose in the following pages.

SHIFTING NEIGHBORHOODS, REVOLVING DOORS

Cardwell Nuckols, one of the authors of this book, was born in 1949 and grew up in Charlottesville, Virginia during the 1950's. He recalls living in a neighborhood where he could safely enter almost any house in a three- or four-block area and ask the mother (who usually stayed at home full-time) for a peanut butter and jelly sandwich. This was a time and place where it was safe to leave doors unlocked and car keys in the ignition.

Those of us who grew up watching the wholesome family sitcoms of the 1950's found a similar reality portrayed on television. Watching "Leave It to Beaver," we saw a father who was usually impeccably dressed, sober, serene, and a productive employee. After a full day of work, he still had enough energy to take care of all the problems between Wally and Eddie. He had enough time to go into the backyard and throw a little ball with the Beaver.

Compare Charlottesville of 1950 to the streets of Watts or the South side of Chicago in 1993. Compare the world of Ward and Wally Cleaver to the families of battered, sexually abused, unparented, and addicted adolescents. The contrast with large sections of present-day America could not be more stark.

The Revolving Door

Even those adolescents who somehow transcend their environments long enough to find their way into treatment face overwhelming odds. After graduating from treatment, many of them return to homes where they are unwanted, or where they are tacitly encouraged to resume using drugs. In some cases they are actively reinforced for doing so. Prime examples are the adolescents of our acquaintance who have made so much money from dealing drugs that their families do not *want* them to stop. Here the families have an economic stake in the drug subculture.

Our work with these young people will be far more powerful if we enter their map of the world and remember a basic fact: They come from communities where drugs are not a problem but a solution. Dealing and using is a way out. Moreover, drugs provide a way to meet all their developmental needs, no matter how unsatisfactorily.

We can temporarily remove these adolescents from their homes and communities, as happens when they enter treatment. Even then, the ties to their aversive environments endure and their worldviews may remain unchanged. While in treatment, many of these young people try to recreate the kind of relationships they saw on the streets and at home.

This fact ignites the rage or fuels the despair of parents, teachers, and treatment professionals. We can temper this by realizing that addicted adolescents in treatment are simply following their "job description"— the rules they learned to survive an aversive environment.

An Inner World of Rage and Hurt

Unparented, addicted, abused, and profoundly alone, addicted adolescents are simply negotiating the world in the only way they know. Elements of their formula for survival are withdrawal, anger, and depression.

Parents and professionals often find it easy to get "hooked" by the "fireworks"—the disruptive behavior many addicted adolescent display. Doing so usually means a fruitless power struggle. Adults who meet anger with anger are fighting on the adolescent's turf and likely to be met with two responses: rage or isolation.

Instead we can define a new place to work with these adolescents. And that is earlier to do when we remember that inside them is a world of hurt. All the bravado we see is meant to convince one audience: themselves. As a working assumption, we take it that the adolescent who comes through the door looking the toughest is the most vulnerable. These young people have a vested interest in shutting us out emotionally, because they fear that their fundamental pain will be discovered.

Is It Possible to Break Through?

Those of us who do manage to get past such defenses have a profound and moving experience. Often we are the first people to glimpse the intellectual and emotional toll that addiction and aversive environments have taken on these adolescents.

One of us spent four years working with incest victims—as many as forty clients at a time. These people were demanding and tough. Yet most of them came to a point—sometimes in one hour, others in six months—where they told the truth about what had happened to them. Every time a therapist reaches that point, we know that something sacred has occurred. Everything in the client's life has militated against establishing such a personal bond; yet the miracle occurs.

When working with addicted adolescents, it can help us to remember that such moments are truly miraculous. We can reflect on how much courage it takes these young people to overcome the fear of rejection and trust any adult enough to enter a healing relationship. This is especially true of adolescents who have known only rejection or abuse at the hands of adults.

They See Few Alternatives to Drugs

It is easy for adults to underestimate the difficulty of convincing addicted adolescents that they have numerous options in life. Take a 15-year-old crack dealer with no vocational skills who has dropped out of high school. He lives in an impoverished, crime-ridden neighborhood, comes from addicted parents, and has no more ability to consider long-range consequences than he did at age eight. Suppose, too, that dealing makes him five hundred dollars per night. What alternative careers can we expect him to genuinely consider? A minimum-wage job at the shopping mall will hardly seem like an attractive offer.

One treatment counselor reveals how intractable the situation can be:

> *Even the dealers that I have talked to who have stayed in high school are staying in for the social status. They can walk around and be one of the big men on campus. One of the kids that I saw wouldn't drop out of high school because it be throwing his business away. All his contacts were there, and he could look good.*
>
> *Tell them about the pitfall of dealing and they'll say, 'Well, my uncle did it and my other cousin does it and they make big money. They're living in a big home out with a Cadillac and a pool or a BMW. They've made it, so why are you telling me that I can't?'*

These are the young people who are supposed to "just say no." Saying that to a 10-year-old who has entered the drug subculture is like telling somebody who is clinically depressed to have a nice day. And when we appeal to these children to participate in athletics and complete homework, we sound equally ludicrous. Making grades and honing social skills take a back seat to more immediate questions: "When I go home, will mom and dad still be fighting? Will anybody even be at home? Is there any food in the house? Maybe I'd better go out and hustle so I can get some dinner tonight." Our appeals that these young people play by the rules and join the system usually fall on deaf ears. After all, the system has failed them, and they are surviving an unbearable situation.

Learning Survival Skills

The developmental deficits of addicted adolescents are real, as we saw in chapter three. Yet it is possible to sell these people short if we consider only their cognitive, emotional, and social immaturity. Addicted adolescents from aversive environments are, often quite literally, survivors. They know how to "hustle," how to get by, how to sell their wares, and how make it out on the streets. Their survival skills are not the skills needed to flourish in school, family life, treatment programs, or the work world. Yet they are evidence of capacity for adaptation and a unique and sophisticated learning style.

FAMILIES

One fundamental element of aversive environments deserves close scrutiny: the addicted adolescent's family.

Disengaged Families

One prominent figure in the study of families is Salvador Minuchin. His work was with inner-city black families has earned him a deserved fame, as does his more recent interest in social change.

Minuchin described two kinds of distressed families. One he called an *enmeshed system*; the other he called a *disengaged system*. In enmeshed families we see a lack of discrete emotional boundaries between members. The boundaries are amoeba-like, with no clear sense of where they begin and end.

In contrast, adolescents from disengaged homes are more likely to be loners. During treatment, these young people are harder to pull into the therapeutic community. And though they are not antisocial, they often appear incapable of close relationships. Perhaps the main reason for this is that they have never been taught how to be in a relationship. Their family environments have provided no models of human caring or understanding. Even the elementary truths of family life—when you hit your sister, it hurts her—may have never been explained to disengaged adolescents. Chances are no one at home paid enough attention to offer such feedback.

Minuchin's distinction between enmeshed and disengaged families is useful in working with addicted adolescents; many of them come from families with these extreme characteristics. In the words of a treatment counselor, "These kids don't come from homes where they sit down at the breakfast table and decide what they are going to do this Saturday—whether to go to Wet n' Wild or a picnic or just do chores."

One more point about disengaged families. Parents in these families are often those who want to stand back while psychologists, addiction counselors, and other professionals solve their childrens' problems. Their attitude can be characterized as: "Fix them and I'll be back to pick them up in a few weeks." Addiction is a problem firmly located within the bounds of their children's skin; as parents, they have little or anything to do with the situation.

Cardwell narrates his experience with such a family:

I saw a family who called me several years ago to work with their son. They thought he might have a problem with crack cocaine. Their initial call came on a Sunday when I was preparing to leave for a trip; I agreed to meet them at the airport for an informal, initial assessment, perhaps a few recommendations.

Mom and dad arrived early, before their son, so I talked with them briefly. Mom's dominant concern seemed to be that she get her money's worth from our session. Dad, it appeared, had some kind of nervous disorder (probably the result of alcohol withdrawal). He was shaking badly and plainly didn't want to be there. He had one foot out the door the whole time.

Soon their son, a drug dealer, drove up in a red Porsche. I looked at mom and dad and asked how their son got such a beautiful car. A dead silence ensued. Mom looked at dad, dad looked at mom, and they looked back at each other. Finally, mom said to me, "Well you know, he must have gotten a part-time job." I was ready to go right to McDonald's! Mom continued to complain, wondering why her kids had to have microwaves in their bedrooms, especially since they could not cook. I suspected they were "nuking" cocaine—manufacturing it right in their rooms. It was obviously happening right there in front of the parents and they refused to look at it.

Differentiation and Family Flexibility

What is a normal family? When discussing family relationships, psychiatrist Murray Bowen used the term *differentiation*. In everyday language we would say that families with a high level of differentiation have clear personal boundaries. Its members are able to empathize with and care for each other. At the same time, they do not have a knee-jerk reaction to each other's anxiety, and their responses to other family members are based on reflection as well as feelings. They share mutual interests but maintain a healthy sense of individuality. Furthermore,

highly differentiated people can be flexible in their behavior and negotiate solutions to problems. Al-Anon's
concept of "detachment with love" shares same of the
same features as differentiation.

At lower levels of differentiation, the family picture
changes. People are more reactive and less reflective.
They cannot tolerate anxiety as well, and family members
base their decisions more on emotion than intellect.

Addicted adolescents often come from enmeshed or
disengaged families that are low in differentiation. In
other words, these adolescents tend to grow up in a
reactive environment where people cannot handle much
anxiety; yet the anxiety is unmistakably there. The reaction
we speak of here may be violent, or it may involve alcohol
or drug use. In either case, it reflects poor problem-solving
skills.

Flexibility is also important here. In a rigid family
system, people have little idea how to manage stress; in
flexible families, just the opposite is true. One important
measure of our mental health is the amount of stress we
can handle skillfully, the number of life problems we can
solve without recourse to violence, rage, depression,
alcohol, or other drugs.

Lack of Parenting

A common scenario in the families of addicted adolescents
is a lack of parenting. Parents may be physically absent;
they may be emotionally disengaged from the family; or
they can cease to be a healthy force in the family because
they spend so many of their waking hours intoxicated.
This typically means that children are forced to take up
the slack and assume the responsibility of caring for
younger siblings. Children as young as six are often caring

for infants because mom is drunk or on a clandestine mission to secure more drugs.

We can describe adolescents who have been forced into this role with terms from the popular literature on codependency. Counselors may describe these young people as rigid and unable to have fun. They often view the world in simplistic, all-or-nothing categories. What's more, they are perfectionistic and highly critical of themselves. It may well seem pointless to confront these adolescents since they already so adept at "beating up on themselves."

These qualities can be barriers to successful recovery from addiction. In treatment, these young people are asked to examine their thoughts and feelings, make amends, or participate in group therapy. For the perfectionistic adolescent, these represent unacceptable risks. Even more routine tasks such as singing songs or writing in a journal may fuel high levels of anxiety. The possibility of being criticized or rejected by peers, or completing a task less than perfectly, is a constant worry.

Survivors Who Still Want a Family

It is almost a cliche to point out how isolated people feel today. Many people lack a solid connection to a religious community, to neighborhoods, co-workers, relatives, and even to our immediate family members. This is one reason for the rapid growth of self-help groups such as those based on the Twelve Steps of Alcoholics Anonymous.

The isolation just mentioned may also explain the powerful appeal of gangs to addicted adolescents. It is possible to see gangs as the families that these young people never had. Gangs represent a group with clear norms and standards for behavior, ruled by leaders who set limits, who define what is acceptable and mandatory. And in the gang there are not only explicit rules but clearly defined consequences for unacceptable behavior.

Adolescents who join these groups at least learn something about the art of relationships—how to bond with other gang members. Gang membership can even indicate the potential for success in drug treatment and lifelong recovery. Adolescents with a conduct disorder, in contrast, are often loners. They fail to form even the kind of alliances we see in gangs.

Gangs and the drug subculture offer ways to fulfill the developmental needs of adolescence. They offer avenues to novelty, power, excitement, sex, and status. In these circles, the people who are seen as "making it" are frequently the pimps and drug dealers. These are realities we must accept before we can offer credible alternatives to addicted adolescents.

Virtually the only thing that can win over these young people is a therapeutic community that displays the characteristics of a truly healthy family. Essentially, this is the atmosphere that is created by successful treatment centers. It is also useful to assume that this atmosphere is what addicted adolescents truly want, even though they rebel against it initially. Yes, there are young people with deep-seated conduct disorders and those who are firmly antisocial. Yet we believe that they are the exceptions. The majority of chronically addicted adolescents can be genuinely drawn to adults and peers who are consistent, available and supportive. We see this in the adolescents who will not let down in front of a group, but who will follow a therapist into an office and begin to open up in a private session. This is a powerful and poignant sign that addicted adolescents want something we can offer.

DUAL DISORDERS

During the last twenty years, we have seen marked increases in the number of adolescents who enter treatment with dual disorders. This term refers to people who are not only chemically dependent but experiencing emotional disturbance or personality disorders as well. These include conduct disorder, attention deficit/hyperactivity disorder, and borderline personality disorder.

Conduct Disorder is Common

The diagnostic criteria for conduct disorder read like a blanket description of many of the chronically addicted adolescents who enter treatment. Conduct disorder is defined as a disturbance of conduct lasting at least six months. Signs of conduct disorder include fire-setting, truancy, running away, stealing, lying, destruction of property, use of weapons, fighting, and other socially unacceptable behavior.

Those who work with addicted adolescents commonly remark that most of their clients enter the door with five or six of these criteria, well beyond the three required for a positive diagnosis.

Adolescents with conduct disorder are "smooth," often adopting a facade that fools us into thinking they can bond with others. The crucial distinction, as one therapist maintains, is between the adolescents who seem capable of empathy and those who do not:

> *What I try to do is understand whether or not they are able to experience remorse, whether or not they can empathize with others. Are they capable of establishing a therapeutic alliance with me? Do I feel there is any*

bonding going on with me or even with any other client? However, a good conduct disordered person is going to be very smooth. Here you may have someone who is very unsocialized, aggressive. And once you put them in jail or probation and through a treatment center or two, they can learn to be more socialized and less aggressive, at least in certain situations. But they still will exploit you. They are still not going to truly bond with you. Their past history is one of few close relationships with anyone—including their immediate family.

Besides being a path to excitement, alcohol and drugs serve another purpose for adolescents with conduct disorder: They are a way to beat the system. They are a way to do treatment instead of "hard time." It is better to take the option of treatment over jail. This option is often offered by the court.

BORDERLINE PERSONALITY DISORDER

The condition called *borderline personality disorder* is a hybrid term. It points to a condition that falls between the milder mental illnesses we call neurosis and the more serious problems we label as psychosis. People with borderline personality disorder may show features of both conditions. Not surprisingly, there is wide disagreement as to what the term really means when applied to any given individual.

We can, however, make some possible generalizations about adolescents who may be described as "borderline." In a sense, the term is ironic, because it conjures up images of a people with clear personal boundaries and a sense of individuality. Yet precisely the opposite is usually true. In reality, these people often have almost amoebic boundaries, much like people from enmeshed families. At times this is expressed in problems with identity. These adolescents may also project their emotions to others. This happens with the person who is visibly angry and approaches a counselor saying, "I think you are angry with me, and I want to talk about it."

Adolescents with borderline personality disorder also display all-or-nothing thinking. Again, their lives are governed by extremes of thought and feeling; people and events are either all good or all bad; feelings are either happy or sad. Ambiguity, moral complexity, and paradox are not parts of their world view.

Adolescents with this disorder may often indulge in "bughouse romances" during treatment and early recovery. This can result from a client's aversions to being alone, combined with an early life history of abusive relationships. These are the people who attend an AA meeting and gravitate toward the most distressed, pathological person in group, firm in the belief that "together we can make it." Typically these relationships are fleeting, lasting perhaps two hours or two weeks before both people relapse into alcohol or other drug use.

Two final notes about this condition. First, in as many as eighty to eighty-five percent of people with borderline personality disorder, we find some type of early trauma. Incest and sexual abuse are common examples.

Some young people with borderline characteristics may also be described as histrionic. This term describes people who are all "hype" and no substance. Often in early life they were rewarded for being cute or for physically overpowering other people. Seldom were they rewarded for being caring or competent. And frequently they grew up in environments where they were expected to be good but never taught how to do so, environments rich in expectations but deficient in skill building and role models.

LEARNING DISABILITIES

Many addicted adolescents enter treatment with learning disabilities. Research indicates that children of alcoholics and addicts can display these problems three to four times as often as children from other families. Especially prevalent is a condition called *attention deficit hyperactivity disorder*.

Attention Deficits Create Problems

Failing to recognize this condition produces a cycle of frustration for the young person, parents, teachers, and treatment staff. For example, asking these clients to complete a task requiring sustained attention can be a ticket to failure. Besides this, adolescents with attention deficit/hyperactive disorders may appear to have conduct disorders. Their disruptive behavior often springs from their inability to handle sensory stimuli. A treatment counselor explains:

> There is one type of kid with attention deficit hyperactivity disorder who really wants to be a part of what is going on in the unit. Yet there are two problems. For one, they just can't handle overstimulation. Once things get too loud, too complicated, or too intense for them, they shut down or just lose it. Even though they feel bad about it later, they might end up throwing somebody off a balcony. They may have an auditory problem or some other problem that does not allow them to deal with a certain level of

stimuli. So they just kind of fritz out, and they are not in total control of that. Second, it's hard for them to concentrate. You tell them to stop a behavior and two seconds later they are at it again. Some of the hyperkinetic behavior and impulsive acting out may be a part of that. Often they're rejected by their peer group and quite lonely.

Interesting enough, adolescents with attention deficit/ hyperactive disorder may have paradoxical or surprising reactions to drugs. We might well expect these young people to be attracted to alcohol and other depressants. Yet we can sometimes find them using powerfully addicting stimulants such as crack. They may even use such drugs to medicate themselves, as with the adolescent who said he used crack to feel calm, and used it only at school. The substance actually helped him to feel more relaxed. Some adults, as well as adolescents, tell us that they slept better after using cocaine.

Adolescents with this condition often have poor coordination. They are frequently described as accident prone, clumsy, and frequent visitors to emergency rooms for broken limbs. Parents may dismiss this behavior as evidence that their children are "spacey" or thoughtless.

These adolescents come into treatment and are given written assignments and reading activities. Sometimes they cannot perform but will not admit it. However, they may have been called "slow," "retards," or "stupid" all their lives and would rather be labeled "resistant" than called "stupid" again. Always be sure that the adolescent can perform the required tasks before giving an assignment. This can be done by asking the adolescent to write two goals for treatment or to read the philosophy of the center and explain it in his or her own words. Do this in private, not before a peer group. If an adolescent cannot complete these tasks, find another way to learn. For example, drawing pictures, watching videos, listening to audio tapes, or verbal communication might allow they to learn the basics needed for recovery.

Solutions

Three imperatives stand out when we ask how to respond to the problems explored in the first two parts of this book. One is to bring chronically addicted adolescents into treatment and begin their path to recovery. Second is to promote the cognitive, intellectual, and social maturity of these young people through bonds with healthy individuals and surrogate families. And third is to change the aversive environments that so deeply influenced these adolescents. Central to the later task is building ties between the adolescent's home environment and the culture of recovery.

These three tasks overlap in countless ways. In this part of the book, we have chosen to group our suggested solutions under two headings: establishing rapport with the adolescent and exploring community-based treatment.

. . . 5

Creating Rapport

It was Milton Erickson, M.D. who described the phenomenon of entering the patient's "map of the world." When we do so we find that many of the problems inherent in clinical treatment of chronically addicted adolescents are better understood.

First of all, it is critically important that the professional understands that how addicts enter treatment, regardless of their motivation, has very little to do with the ultimate outcome.

Secondly, the addictions professional must be able to accept where the addicted adolescent is at any particular moment in treatment. This includes a thorough understanding of defense systems, the addiction's organicity, and the addict's biochemical makeup, all of which have such a strong impact on in-treatment behavior.

And third, ask the question: If the addiction professional cannot enter or understand where the cocaine addict is coming from, how will the addict be led elsewhere? Addiction professionals are well versed in Old Style, Michelob, Jim Beam, Valium and Librium, but are intimidated by such expressions as "beaming up," "going to see Scotty," "Captain Kirkin'," "smoking geek," "copping an eight ball," "pancakes," "crack," "rock," "batu,' "glass" and "ice." If, moreover, the adolescent crack and ice addict adopts a strongly narcissistic posture—as so often happens—the helping person is sometimes even more confused and threatened.

REALITY CONTACT

In considering an intervention with the crack and ice addict, it is very important to understand the "job description" of this addict. The addict has a regressed personality secondary to his use of crack, ice and other substances. This regressed personality has estranged him from himself. In other words, it is in the crack and ice addict's job description not be in touch with the reality.

As stated by David Shapiro (1989), "the neurotic person is estranged from his own reason because those reasons themselves are subject to conflict. He is estranged from his own reasons by reactions and prejudices of which he is also unaware; often he is not even sympathetically disposed to understand that he has his reasons. We, however, are outside his conflict and his particular prejudices and this is our great advantage in helping him." Shapiro's remarks apply to adolescent crack or ice addicts because they are estranged from reality.

If, in our initial treatment, we press the adolescent addict to get in touch with his feelings, he quite often incapable of this type of introspection. In other words, the adolescent has developed an addictive ego that is surrounded by psychological defense systems to such a point that he is estranged from himself. There is a morbid personality in play here that can be described as the addicted ego. It is involved in a dyadic struggle with the

"I." The addicted ego is in control and part of the task of working with an adolescent addict is getting him in touch with the real self. This, however, takes time.

Allow for Cognitive Impairment

Always remember that moderate to high dose crack and ice use will precipitate paranoia. The combination of paranoia, along with a thought-process problem, can cause difficulty in the initial interaction. Also remember that in order to support the habit, the addict has had to participate in illegal behaviors. Therefore, the therapist may tend to see a paranoid individual who is cognitively impaired, who does not trust you and often does not want to self-disclose.

Paranoia, in the form of exaggerated suspiciousness and hypervigilance, will hinder the therapeutic alliance. When we combine this paranoia with the illegal acts so commonly committed by the crack and ice addict, an unwillingness to self-disclose is typically present. In recovery, we are asking the adolescent addict to change everything and change it quickly. Their job description is to maintain their lover—the drug—at all costs.

Avoid Early Labeling

An interventionist stated, "The grandiosity is there because the cocaine addict has that immediate gratification. I have not yet done one cocaine intervention where the person hasn't said, "I already quit." They will sit there loaded, and I know that they are loaded and they say, "I have got it handled." They've truly believed that they got the drug handled. It is very difficult for the cocaine addict to understand that the drug is handling them, until they start hitting the hospital." Remember that the job description of the crack and ice addict is to truly protect their drug. From the perspective of a regressed personality that is well defended, the above statements can be easily understood.

The technique of not labeling the addict or trying to sell the addict on long-term treatment in the first few moments of the intervention is critical. It is much better to get them out of a situation such as a family setting, the criminal justice setting or a work place setting and into an environment that may allow them to back down. If they are labeled too quickly or confronted too hard, the insult may cause them to "numb off" or to hit the ceiling. From the interventionist's perspective, it is very difficult to convince a family member after the crack and ice addict has stormed out of the room that the first seeds of recovery had just been laid. It is typically a much better strategy to work towards getting the person to someone who can properly assess them.

By not labeling too early, the crack and ice addict's integrity remains intact. Once the crack or ice addict has reached a treatment setting we may have a better possibility of motivating them towards treatment. However, there are situations where hard line confrontations may be helpful with the crack and ice addict. Often in cases of chronic recidivism or with individuals who may have more of a power/control, street-oriented, approach to life, a more directive approach may be mandated.

A Therapist's Personal Qualities are Critical

It is empathy and other personal qualities of the therapist that are so critically important. Research has shown that a patient's judgement of the personal qualities of a therapist is a better indicator of outcome than the therapist's training and theoretical background.

Robert Millman, M.D. (1986) writes "the major issues in the initial stages of therapy with all patients is developing a productive relationship; this is often quite difficult to do with substance abusers. Patients are often openly hostile to treatment, they deny the presence of the extent of the problem, they have had repeated treatment failures and they have lost control of the drug use."

It is critical, at this stage, that the therapist enter into a relationship with an attitude of acceptance and have the innate ability of empathy. It will be the therapeutic relationship, established with empathy between the addiction professional and the adolescent addict, that will be the best and most consistent determinant of outcome.

Acknowledge the Addict's Profound Isolation

All crack and ice addicts reach that time is their existence where they are alone and feel isolated. It is that existential vacuum that is part of the motivational pain that responsible for some of the initial movement toward recovery. Later in recovery, the existential issues of loneliness and isolation will often be expressed as a sense of boredom.

You Must Understand Cocaine

In regard to street intelligence, knowledge of the drug scene and other variables associated with drug use, the addicts themselves must be considered the experts. Both alcoholics and drug addicts appear to be extremely sensitive to and instantly aware of the therapist's sophistication or lack thereof in regards to their drug of choice.

One way of understanding the potential interaction at this stage is through the following metaphor.

Let's imagine that I am the best alcoholism therapist in your part of the country. Let's also imagine that you are a poor suffering alcoholic and you enter into my office seeking some help for your disorder. You look at me and say, "I went out and had some Wild Turkey last night, but hey, there are a lot of people worse off than I am." If, as a therapist, I look at you and say "Wild Turkey . . . it's something you drink, isn't it?"

How am I doing so far in terms of establishing rapport? If you had any brain cells left, you would exit the room, or, if you decided to stay, you would know at once that you had a psychological advantage over me in regard to my lack of understanding of alcoholism.

Now, let's further consider the metaphor. You are the best stimulant addiction therapist in your part of the country. I am a poor suffering crack or ice addict. I enter your door and say, "Yeah, I have used crack and ice a few times, but it is really no problem. I have been drinking and smoking marijuana for years and never have had any difficulty at all. I have never lost control. Sure I went out and copped a few bottles and hit the stem, but don't tell me I am an addict." You, as the therapist, look at me stupefied and reply . . .?

It is the quality of this initial interaction that will have a lot to do with the rapport that is established between the adolescent crack and ice addict and the addiction professional. It is very important that addiction professionals understand the nature of stimulant drugs, how they impact on the neurological systems and, how this is manifest in a psychobehavioral fashion.

It is also important to understand some of the street jargon and, to have questions that you might ask such as:

"Did you make the rock or did you buy it already made? What kind of pipe did you smoke your ice in? Have you ever had times when you became paranoid and paced back and forth thinking that every little sound was a police officer? Have you even sold bottles?" An articulation of these and other universal experiences of crack and ice addicts will indicate to the addict that you have entered his experience.

Use "Care-frontation," Not Confrontation

In order to establish empathy with the adolescent cocaine and ice addict, a therapist must be able to go beyond the external narcissistic presentation, while always observing the heart of the patient. The heart and soul of the crack and ice addict is filled with hurt, fear and loss. However, it may take time to establish a therapeutic relationship that will allow the therapist to get close to that hurt. Narcissistic personalities will typically keep others at a distance. They prefer superficial relationships.

Therefore, the role of the interventionist may be more collaborative or as a consultant. This stance is the opposite of taking a hard line, confrontational approach. The clinician must remember that the goal of the intervention is to get the crack and ice addict to the dance (i.e., some form of treatment) and not necessarily to establish *immediate* rapport and to label the individual an addict, alcoholic, junkie or other term that may be perceived negatively by the crack and ice addict.

Often, however, the adolescent crack and ice addict gives the therapist what's needed to engage in a process that may lead to treatment. The following dialogue between therapist and addict illustrates both the goal of getting the addict into treatment and how to handle a type of psychological defense presented by the crack and ice addict.

Tell me what brought you here today.

I was told that I had a problem with drugs. Hell, everybody I know uses drugs. I have been drinking alcohol for years and have never had a problem with alcohol. I think these people are crazy.

Well, tell me about your use of drugs.

Well, it is true that I have done crack cocaine several times and have tried ice. But look, I am not an addict. I don't use everyday. And like I told you, I don't have any problem with any other drugs and I have been drinking for a long time.

Well, you know, you may be right. Maybe you don't have a problem with other drugs, but sometimes with drugs like crack and ice, there is more going on than we think. Therefore, what I would like to do is refer you to the best addictionologist in the whole area. As a matter if fact, this person is one of the most famous addictionologists in the country. I would like for the two of you to sit down together this afternoon. I will arrange the appointment right now. In a confidential session, both of you can figure this thing out.

In the above dialogue, we have neither used hard confrontation nor have we labeled the individual an addict. As a matter of fact, the therapist "bought into" or aligned with the addict's value system by agreeing that maybe there was no other drug problem. The goals here is to get the crack and ice addict where they may become influenced by the process of treatment.

Allow for Short-Term Rewards

Another powerful technique for working with adolescents and immature adults is focusing on short-term rewards. Ask such clients to complete a traditional goal in treatment, such as remaining abstinent for one year, and they are likely to feel they've been given a life sentence. Many of these clients comes to us with a low frustration tolerance and little sense of the long-range consequences of their actions. What's more, they are used to relieving any psychological discomfort with a drug that delivers bliss in anywhere from a few minutes to a few seconds. For people who live with this map of the world, one year—even one day—sounds like infinity. Hence the traditional AA slogan "One Day At a Time" may simply not speak to them.

One key to motivating addicted adolescents in treatment, then, is helping them realize the dream of recovery in small, concrete steps. These clients need a concrete sense of accomplishment and frequent rewards. Every day on the treatment unit, they must accomplish a small segment of the overall goal, putting in place a single piece of the recovery puzzle. Instead of presenting them with one-year or one-week tasks, we are well-advised to give them hour-by-hour or even second-by-second assignments.

One application of this approach is posing a simple question to the addicted adolescent: "How many seconds have you been straight?" At 86,400 seconds a day, and a quarter of a million seconds in three days, the numbers are substantial. Such a perspective can be highly empowering to people who are used to negotiating life on a moment-by-moment basis.

Get Dealers in Touch with Their Pain

Arguing the virtues of a drug-free lifestyle with a 15-year-old drug dealer who makes $150,000 per year presents a formidable challenge. This is especially true for underpaid treatment professionals who find themselves taking on two jobs just to survive.

Here a useful tactic is to dealers vividly in touch with their pain. And we can be assured that anyone who is immersed in the violence and emotional wreckage of the drug and gang subcultures has plenty of pain for us to work with.

One thing we can do is point out how much they are like users. It's a fact that the dealer needs drugs just as much as addicted users do. Dealers, too, obsess over drugs and go to great lengths to protect their supply. If that supply is threatened, then dealers are likely to panic, much like alcoholics who find themselves with an empty liquor cabinet.

We can also make the point that dealers are not simply purveying drugs—they are dealing in death. To begin, they are often dealing physical death to their customers who are addicts. Beyond that, they are trading is spiritual death as well. In a fundamental and profound way, dealing means valuing dead things over living things. One treatment counselor puts the issue succinctly:

I ask the dealers: Why are you selling the drugs, what do you want? Well, they say, I want the money and that is something. But what do you want the money for, I respond? It's for jewelry, for a house, for a car, for guns—

all for things that are not alive. It's all dead stuff. Jewelry you get out of the ground, and then you take that dead stuff and you put it on and you choose that over the well being of somebody who is alive. You are choosing that dead stuff over people.

If these kids feel some remorse over this fact, we can ask them to talk about what they really want. Many of their answers center on power, control, prestige. And what they really want is self-esteem. I guide them to see that there are other ways of getting that—ways that don't mean killing people and accumulating dead stuff. This opens the door to the possibility of recovery.

Help Clients Develop Empathy

Treatment success stories illustrate a basic need for the adolescent to develop empathy. The word "empathy" derives from the German *einfuhlung*, which means "feeling oneself into" someone or something. The early use of the term often had to do with the observer's response to the expressive quality of a work of art. It was soon expanded, to include responses not only to works of art, but to individuals.

Currently when talking about empathy, the therapist relates to the sharing of moods and feelings. Leslie Brothers, M.D. (1989) gives an example of empathy when he talks about a man at a dinner party finding that the people seated on each side of him had turned away and are conversing with their neighbors. As this is going on, the individual seated in the middle then contrives to look as though there is nothing wrong, that he is very much at ease and enjoying himself contemplating some flower arrangement in the middle of the table. Brothers talks about the character's complex emotional state, a mixture of loneliness and wish to alleviate discomfort. This emotional states has been experienced by many who can in turn empathize with that similar situation.

A second order of empathy involves the capacity to understand and reflect changes in a person's life. For example, if the first person to help the crack or ice addict points out to the addict the tremendous strength and courage it must have taken to come the point where he decided to come in and at least take a look at his problem, the process of empathy to a higher order has occurred.

From an existential perspective, the initial therapeutic goal must be to engage the patient with the living. This has much more to do with empathy and love than with trying to label the patient. Acceptance of where they are in the "here and now" is imperative. It is not helpful to make a remark such as "but look at what you have to live for."

If we are not allied with the adolescent addict at this moment of pain then we will not be able to establish the therapeutic alliance that will be an important motivational factor during the early recovery process. It is the sensitivity and recognition, along with the empathy for the desperate situation of the addict at this moment in life, that will be so important in helping to rekindle or respark the life that exists within.

Start From Where Clients are Today

Another crucial goal for addicted adolescents is gaining something few of them have ever had: self-esteem. And we can help adolescent develop this quality by simply acknowledging where they stand in the present.

A story about the therapist Milton Erickson makes this point. Erickson once had a client named Herman, a man who began therapy by saying to Erickson, "I am just a moron. No one can ever love me." Erickson's response was something like this: "You know, you are right. You really are a moron. But in terms of our goals in therapy, let's try to make you the best moron you can possibly be."

"As a moron," Erickson continued, "you are probably not going to be a brain surgeon or a rocket scientist or anything like this. You will probably have to be a carpenter, maybe a landscaper. When you think about it, you really have to be coordinated to be a good moron. And to help you be the best moron you can be I want you to take dancing lessons. That will help you learn better hand-eye coordination so you can really hit a hammer or use that shovel a little bit better."

After Herman completed dancing lessons, Erickson congratulated him and said, "You are becoming quite a competent moron. In order to test whether or not you have really achieved your goal, I am going to give you a test. During this test, if no one notices that you are a moron, then we will know that you have truly succeeded. On Saturday night there is a barn dance here in town. You are going to go to this barn dance. What you'll probably see there is a lot of women sitting on one side of the room and a lot of men on the other side of the room, all them pretty uncomfortable. What I want you to do is go in and pick out three of those women who are sitting on their side of the wall and dance with them. If none of them figures out that you are a moron, then you have become such a skilled moron that it will be time to discharge you."

Herman succeeds at this assignment, too, finding himself enjoying the dance while most of the other men seem miserable. Soon afterwards, Herman returns to Erickson and he says, "You know Dr. Erickson, I just realized that maybe I wasn't as bad off as I thought."

This story illustrates how we can enter someone else's world and help them cast reality in a new light. It is important to see the irrational, sometimes hostile, behavior through a different pair of glasses. These behaviors are learned coping and survival skills. This is how they survived the crazy violent world around them. This is the continuing task we face in establishing rapport with addicted adolescents, leading them to a sense of possibility that embraces recovery.

... 6

Community-Based Recovery

$\mathbf{B}$ecause of the illegal nature of crack and ice, as well as the tremendous expense of maintaining the drug habit, adolescent crack and ice addicts will often enter a drug culture. This creates a difficult, yet interesting, dilemma for the therapist.

VanDusen and Sherman (1974) describe this dilemma as follows: "The client tends to play out the only ways he knows: to try to manipulate the situation and the therapist to gain satisfaction. In complete contrast, what the therapist really wants is the client who will search out his individual dynamics to gain insight. After some disappointment the therapist finds him not a suitable client. Psychotherapists have tended to reject these people. Conventional psychotherapy is more important for drug dependent individuals who are not in the drug culture, i.e. a housewife or businessman who does not associate with drug users." This is the main reason that conventional psychotherapy is not a solution for addicted adolescents. In many communities there is just no apparent alternative or way out for adolescents involved in the drug culture.

We must, again, ask that most telling of questions: What do we have to offer this adolescent or young adult?

What do we have that they want? If we cannot answer these questions, we cannot expect treatment to solve the total problem. Treatment can do an excellent job of preparing the adolescent addict for transition and reintegration into the community. But, if the community has nothing to offer the individual, there will be very little long-term change. Crack and ice addicts recognize this better than anyone else. This hopelessness is a natural response for them as they return to the streets or to the schools after being in a treatment program and see no one around them recovering.

COMMUNITY-BASED TREATMENT

David Smith and Darrell Inaba know a lot about community based pretreatment, based on their work with addicts and alcoholics in the Tenderloin District of San Francisco. They studied the population and projected that if the crack epidemic continues from 1990 to the year 2000, ninety percent of Afro-American males age fifteen to twenty-five would have aids, be crack addicted, or in jail.

An example of how the drug subculture and cultural perspectives have been used to promote recovery way, is found in a technique described to the author by Daryl Inaba of the Haight-Asbury Clinic in San Francisco. Dr. Inaba describes a phenomenon called "Hubba Day."

Hubba Day is the first and fifteenth of the month in a certain section of San Francisco, called the Tenderloin District. The Tenderloin District is a notorious crack cocaine infested area where there are many single mothers who are exploited by drug dealers. This exploitation takes place on "Mother's Day," which is the first and middle day of the month—when the mothers get their checks. Drug dealers are typically not far behind.

The church in this neighborhood is a wellspring of strength within the community. All the mothers will gather there in the morning on the first and fifteenth of the month, with a sense of unity and mission. The mission is to go in groups to gather their checks and to pay bills and buy groceries for their children. The group strength allows them to accomplish these goals. At the end of the day they come back to the church to celebrate the completion of another Hubba Day.

Within this description given by Dr. Inaba, we see the role of cultural beliefs involving the church. We also see the power of unity, the bringing together of people with a common bond and mission. We also see the potential for exploitation by the drug subculture within the environment.

There is a certain beauty about this. This is an extension of what we are trying to do. Its an opportunity to get high and stay high together, to socialize in a recovery-oriented way. To have a dream and to pull it off.

Know the Community

Enter the addict's culture on two levels. It is not imperative that all staff members working with crack and ice addicts come from the street or have backgrounds with the criminal justice system. It is imperative, however, that people working with addicts know something about addicts who have a history of street involvement and a history of criminal activity.

There are two particular cultural interactions at play here. Number one is the cultural background of the individual. Addicts may come from a Afro-American,

Hispanic or Caucasian background. They may be Asian, European or Appalachian. The other type of culture has to do with the street culture or the drug culture that interacts with the ethnoculture of that particular community. The therapist or treatment program leadership must understand both. It is a matter of finding the strengths within these cultures that will allow the individual to have the best chance at recovery, to become involved with the positive, recovering-supporting elements in the community.

Avoid stereotyping communities. Although the sketch of Hubba Day does not begin to reveal the depth of wisdom that went into this particular intervention, it does describe what can be termed an ethnographic survey. An ethnographic survey involves going into a community and looking for its strengths and then using those strengths in the treatment planning and intervention process. If we plan treatments from weakness, we are perpetuating failure.

While each culture and community has strengths, we must be careful not to respond to stereotypes. The strengths that might be found in the Afro-American population in the Tenderloin District of San Francisco, may be different than the strengths found in a similar group in a different neighborhood within the same city. A Caucasian community in Kansas City may have one set of strengths while another Caucasian community that lives on the other side of town may have different sets of standards and strengths that need to be understood.

There is a metaphor describing this process. It goes like this: There is an old man standing on the side of a hill minding his own business. One day a stranger or wanderer from another town comes by and says to the old man, "Please tell me about those people in that city below."

The old man looks at the stranger and says, "Sir, I will be happy to do this, but first tell me from where you come."

The stranger then relates a story of where he comes from. He says, "Where I come from people do not respect one another. The are very hostile and violent and they will kill you. People where I come from have no respect for human dignity and no value for life at all. Where I come from is probably the worst place in America."

The old man looks at the stranger and says, "You know, you will find those same types of people in that city below."

The next day this old man is standing on the hill again, looking down at the little town, when another stranger or comes by. The stranger looks at the old man and says, "Old man, please tell me about those people in that city below."

Well, the old man looks at the stranger and says, "Sir, I will be very happy to do that, but first tell me from where you come."

"Where I come from, people really care about each other. There is very little they will not do to help you along the way. Where I come from people are truly loving and giving. It just brings tears to my eyes to think about having to leave there. My town is probably the best place in America and the people within this town are probably the best people in America."

The old man looks at the stranger and says, "You know, you will find exactly those kinds of people in that city below."

The Role of Self-Help Groups

For a continuing care model to work, some form of supportive family or surrogate situation must be put into place. There are several possibilities when we talk about surrogate extensions of the family. Within the context of community, we will look at three aspects that contribute to recovery or relapse. These three aspects are self-help, church, and family.

According to the Twelve Steps and Twelve Traditions (1953), "Alcoholics especially should be able to see that instinct run wild in themselves is the underlying cause of their destructive drinking. We have drunk to drown feelings of fear, frustration and depression. We have drunk to escape the feeling of guilt and passions, and then have drunk again to make more passions possible. We have drunk for vain glory. . . ." Be it an alcoholic, crack addict or any other addict, the message is the same: A life out of control; a life on the brink of disaster.

It is the second step of Alcoholics Anonymous that states, ". . . came to believe that a power greater than ourselves could restore us to sanity." Alcoholic's Anonymous, Narcotic's Anonymous or any self-help group could be substituted for a higher power. Step Two is in essence a rallying point for sanity. It is also the opportunity to straighten out relationships with the God of our choice. The grief process of recovery is so well documented in the steps of these powerful programs. Step One, stating, "We admitted we were powerless over alcohol—that our lives had become unmanageable." Even Step Three, ". . . made a decision to turn our will and our lives over to the care of God as we understood him," is imperative to the process of acceptance and surrender. This step relates to the misuse of will power and how it is an enslaving and entrapping concept in recovery.

These are but a few examples of the synergy that exists between treatment and self-help. Both treatment and self-help are powerful when they stand alone. Combining the two creates a chance for recovery that is better than either alone.

Some of the leading minds of our era have suggested that a close working relationship with the anonymous groups will enhance treatment success. Brown and Yalom (1977), for example, were concerned that a more conflictual psychotherapy group would not yield the necessary acceptance needed by the alcoholic. They found that the problem could be resoled by encouraging group members to obtain help from Alcoholic's Anonymous. There they would receive the total support necessary for their recovery.

Brown and Yalom were concerned that there might be conflict when an individual attended two different types of groups. This concern was resolved by pointing out that group psychotherapy and AA served two separate, but equally necessary, functions. These functions were both vital to their recovery. Flores (1988) states, "There are things that AA can give the members that the group can't and visa versa. The issue of dependency provides an excellent example. AA, by nature of its format, tends to gratify dependency needs. New members are encouraged to rely on AA, on the other members and on a 'higher power' to remain abstinent. The therapy group, on the other hand, satisfies dependency needs only enough to keep the patient in therapy."

In sum, there are differences between the two approaches, but both are designed to be active regimens geared toward facilitating abstinence from alcohol and drugs. Flores goes on to state, "Therapy groups are specifically oriented to a global symptom reduction through the specific use of behavioral and psychological prescriptions and techniques, while AA is regimented towards addressing one specific component of recovery (i.e., abstinence)."

Self-help meetings such as Alcoholic's Anonymous, Narcotics Anonymous and Cocaine Anonymous are part of the behavioral foundation of recovery. Along with physical exercise, nutrition and professional treatment, self-help allows one to break some of the old addictive behavior patterns. A self-help recovery program has very important behavioral ramifications. The concept of socialization in an abstinence atmosphere, in the presence of positive role models, is very important in shaping early abstinence beliefs.

Satisfying Needs for Novelty, Excitement

The adolescent addict will typically desire some degree of excitement in recovery. Although a meeting cannot approximate the artificial euphoria of drugs, there are certainly exciting qualities about self-help programs. Wherever possible, self-help programs—and contact made through these programs—should link recovering crack and ice addicts up with individuals who share common concerns and interests. If these interests are exciting, yet recovery-oriented, a substitute for the excitement of drugs can sometimes be found.

For example, there was an addict who every week would tell his therapist what he knew his therapist would not allow him to do. (The therapist would typically allow him to do what he asked for but reframe it in a positive recovery-oriented fashion.) One day this patient walked into the therapist's office and said, "I know I've got you this time. You will never allow me to do this. I want to go skydiving." The therapist then said, "I think skydiving is a wonderful idea. Just remember that there are two rules.

First, you have to take lessons and second, you must wear a parachute."

Within a weeks a small skydiving club was established. All members of this skydiving club were recovering through the self-help programs of Narcotics Anonymous and Alcoholics Anonymous. They met every Sunday morning at an AA breakfast. After the breakfast they would go to a small airfield and work out together. When they had the money, they would go up in a plane and skydive. Standing in the door, getting ready to jump out of that small airplane was, in may ways, similar to taking a hit off the pipe. It was those moments where they did not have the money to skydive that were frightening. They would lie in the freefall area and watch people freefall towards them.

Another good example of using self-help and the self-help connection to satisfy the need for excitement can be found in the recovering motorcycle group called the Fifth Chapter. Here, individuals can still wear their colors and ride their Harleys or other brand-name motorcycle. Yet members of the Fifth Chapter are all recovering. This activity has allowed them to continue to get some of the features of the motorcycle gang that were very exciting and fulfilling, while staying within the context of a group of people interested in abstinence and recovery.

The self-help groups offer combinations of excitement and socialization on many levels. From sharing at a meeting to being involved in recovery-oriented dances and sports activities, a sense of connectedness in abstinence can emerge.

Bond Addicts to New "Families" Carefully

The importance of utilizing the self-help movement, sponsorship and self-help-related activities to help the adolescent addict find value and meaning cannot be understated. If youthful recovering addicts state that they cannot find anyone similar to them, as crazy as they are or interested in the same things they are interested in, the fact is they have just not looked.

There is no doubt that the self-help group represents a family experience to the recovering addict. Remember that their past family experiences may be been of the dysfunctional variety. They have either been extremely disengaged or enmeshed in their old family situations. Now they have entered different family arrangements. They have entered the treatment family. This entry into the recovering family will be influenced greatly by their primary family. Their attitudes towards group leaders and the role they assume in the group will be very much shaped by their experiences at home.

So, too, will the family haunt the self-help group. The addict will reenact early family scripts in the group. This is important to understand since early in recovery, if left to their own guide, the recovering addict may pick a sponsor, for example, that best represents an internalized parental figure. If this parental figure had a negative impact on their early upbringing, then this figure may also have a negative impact on recovery.

Finding an appropriate meeting for each addict is crucial. For example, sending a crack or ice addict to an Alcoholics Anonymous meeting that may only want to admit those who are primary alcoholics could be a set up for disaster. If it is one of the first self-help encounters for the recovering addict, it may turn out to be extremely negative. At this stage of recovery, these small negative experiences are generalized. The crack and ice addict may then feel that self-help is not for them.

Another important consideration is the therapist's role in being proactive regarding sponsorship. It is believe that early in recovery the therapist should take an active role in helping to pick out or at least screen potential sponsors. A most dramatic example of what can go wrong can be observed in the movie *Clean and Sober*. The principal character,played by Michael Keaton, goes to his first AA meeting and is told to pick a sponsor. He immediately walks up to the most attractive woman in the group and asks her to be his sponsor.

The role of choosing the right sponsor and the right self-help situation is well described by Wallace (1989). Wallace states, "In addition to positive reinforcement, AA in action is consistent with other behavior modification procedures. Recent trends in social learning theory approaches to behavioral change are evident in AA. Models who display patterns and behavior useful in imitative learning and who dispense social reinforcers directly are abundant. Moreover, these models possess attributes that encourage identificatory learning. They are successfully recovering alcoholics themselves and, hence, are regarded as possessing knowledge, expertise, and practical skills useful to newcomers in the program."

Often therapists experience a controversy regarding which meetings are right for an addict. The choice typically is between AA (Alcoholics Anonymous) and NA (Narcotics Anonymous). In the communities where CA (Cocaine Anonymous) exists, there is a third option. Many therapists feel that CA is so early in its development, that there is not enough good recovery to warrant referral. Therefore, by sending a crack or ice addict to Cocaine

Anonymous, the addict may experience a lack of modeling and a precipitation of craving. This has, on many occasions, been the case. The line of thinking that the therapist should take should be based upon strength. In other words, which self-help meetings in your community are the best established, have the best long term sobriety, and offer the best comparison or match-up between their clients and their recovery needs.

Most adolescent addicts are polydrug users. They have had histories of abusing alcohol, marijuana and other self-administered drugs. In this case, most of the self-help groups would be appropriate. Therefore, choose the groups that have the greatest strength to offer the client. Try several of the self-help groups and see which ones work best with youthful members. For example, the crack and ice addict may like Narcotic's Anonymous or Cocaine Anonymous because of the crowd of people and the language that is spoken. Early in recovery they may closely identify with this population of people.

If the therapists insists on AA involvement also, then a very valuable platform has been laid. It has been found that many crack and ice addicts, as their recovery continues, may opt for an Alcoholic's Anonymous program because of the solid recovery that can typically be found within this self-help movement. Also, it is important to consider the fact that no matter where the crack and ice addict goes, they should be able to find an Alcoholic's Anonymous group that will meet their needs. This cannot be said, to date, about Narcotic's Anonymous and Cocaine Anonymous. Also understand that Narcotic's Anonymous in many areas has established incredible strength through growth. In the coming years, Cocaine Anonymous may establish the same strength through growth.

If there is a difficulty facing the therapist in regard to choosing self-help groups, it may have less to do with which group to choose from and more to do with this question: Is there a group that matches well with the client? In the past, it could be said that Alcoholics Anonymous was a white male, middle class, self-help organization. Fortunately, this is shifting.

There are communities in areas where strong self-help is unavailable. At the present, thirty percent of the membership of Alcoholics Anonymous is female. Crack and ice addiction represent a more equal opportunity illness. It is not atypical to find that thirty to forty percent of crack and ice addicts in treatment are female. There also has been proliferation of Afro-American, Hispanic and other ethnic oriented self-help groups. However, the supply of meetings has not met the demand in many areas.

It is often the role of the therapist and the treatment institution to assist in the development of self-help meetings in communities. One way of establishing this is through a volunteer alumni organization. A second way may be to start a hospital and institution first-step oriented meeting using some healthy, happily recovering members of Alcoholics Anonymous or Narcotics Anonymous. These members should have some experience with street drugs, such as crack or ice. With their grounding in recovery they can then start a Narcotics Anonymous or Cocaine Anonymous meeting that can be splintered into communities where there are people struggling with issues of abstinence. Treatment does have to take some responsibility for assisting in the networking process and the establishment of recovering communities. A positive relationship between treatment and self-help best facilitates this relationship.

The Addict and Self-Help Communities

Self-help works for one simple reason: It is a way of life. This way of life is a healthy, productive, abstinence-driven way of life that directly opposes the old addictive, out-of-control, lifestyle.

However, self-help organizations do far more than give the individual the initiative to achieve and sustain abstinence. In essence, Alcoholics Anonymous, Narcotics Anonymous and Cocaine Anonymous can give the youthful addict a chance to participate in a family. This family may be their first opportunity to be in a functional surrounding. Remember that this functional surrounding has at its origin the pure goal of obtaining abstinence.

Again, abstinence is a way of life, not a fad. The reason many diets do not work is that they are faddish. The individual has a goal of losing ten pounds. Once the ten pounds is lost, the goal has been achieved. Therefore, the individual starts to think that maybe they deserve a reward or maybe their weight can now fluctuate. Alcoholics Anonymous, Narcotics Anonymous and Cocaine Anonymous are not like that. Cocaine addiction and amphetamine addiction are life long illnesses. Recovery responds well to life long programs that create and model the abstinent way of life.

Churches in Community Recovery

There is an interesting question that can be asked. Where in town are their buildings that are occupied only at certain hours of the week? Where in town are their groups of people who are capable of giving hope and understanding to the down-trodden? Where in town is there the possibility of exerting the most positive recovery influence, especially in areas where addiction is a problem? What group in town can exert the strongest counterforce against drug dealers and street gangs? A counterforce not of violence, but a counterforce of recovery and hope. The answer all these questions is: the church.

Churches have allowed their space to be used for self-help meetings, but this is not nearly enough. One of the crucial concerns with the treatment of adolescent is that there is not enough treatment available. Today, in many urban areas for example, large numbers of addicts seeking help have no place to go. Would it not be possible to train individuals in general therapy skills and to utilize the church as not only a place of worship, but also a place of hope and recovery? There is probably no more active role that the church could take in helping the community than being a part of recovery for the great numbers of people who are suffering from addiction.

Data relates that one out of eight Americans is suffering from some form of chemical dependency. This may be alcoholism, illicit drug use or abuse of prescription medications. Possibly even more alarming is the fact that every addict impacts negatively on five to eight other people. This includes all of their family members. It has also been said that one in three children coming to school for the first time is crucially impaired by alcoholism or drug abuse. Certainly, this same data not only applies to the general population, but to the church attending population.

According to Stephen Apthorp (1988), "the number of ministers scarred by substance abuse that are seeking to help parishioners who bear the same scars is surprisingly high. In regional training seminars I have conducted for denominational clergy and lay leaders, a show of hands has indicated that eighty-eight percent of clergy present have come from families debilitated by substance abuse and they were aware that it had drastically harmed them. For many, this history was a determining factor in their decision to enter the ministry—hope of the Lord's salvation, as it were."

Impaired pastors often accumulate impaired parishioners. It is well known among therapists that people who grow up in chemically dependent families have a tendency to attract others from similar environments. Apthorp goes on to state, "No wonder that the church at large and the clergy in particular have difficulty recognizing and dealing with today's epidemic affliction of addiction. The church and its leaders are clearly among the afflicted, if not the addicted." In a letter to the editors of a magazine for adult children of alcoholics, the following was confessed:

I have realized that throughout my ministry I have accepted calls to congregations that replicate the dynamics of the alcoholic family in which I was raised. This insight . . . has helped me to discover why my career has be so chaotic.

However, the church is often the first line of defense. Because of the trust the parishioners have in key church staff, especially the minister, a chance for early intervention exists. Either the family or the addicted individual may first come to the priest before they seek any form of help from a professional therapist. This puts the church in the optimal position for some form of prevention or intervention activity. Cairns (1990) discusses the example of ministry in which prevention is perceived as a long-term solution. He describes offering annual educational events on the prevention of substance abuse. Apthorp discusses the fact that congregations do not even observe this one consciousness-elevating Sunday. This is the case because their priest deny the need for alcohol and drug education within the church. Apthorp goes on to state, "In those churches that do promote it (the alcohol and drug aware-ness Sunday) many of the members that have been affected by some substance abuse are not able to under-stand the one-shot message, much less discern how to help themselves. The cycle of denial continues uninterrupted."

Cairns does give two activities that would seem to be very helpful. The first is called a spiritual support group. The purpose of this type of group is to provide spiritual and social support through religious fellowship. It must be remembered that this does not take the place of professional treatment, but can be very helpful to the individual reintegrating back into the community, especial-ly in areas where church and religion are perceived as a strength. Cairns also discusses what he called "Partners in Recovery." People recovering from addictions, such as crack and ice addiction, need wise and loving friends. Typically, adolescent addicts and their families do not have acquaintances who are not heavy drug and alcohol users. When they come out of a treatment program, they will be faced with building a new network of friends who will encourage and support their abstinence.

The Partners in Recovery program establishes a network of good friends who can be a bridge to sanity and spiritual rebirth. It is certainly not enough for the minister to tell an addicted adolescent to just pray harder. This intervention would be analogous to telling someone suffering from a heart attack to pray harder and that the infarction will go away, all the while withholding medical technology.

Many adolescent and young adult addicts have had early upbringing that involved some exposure to principals of a church. The guilt and shame attached to behaviors secondary to their addiction will sometimes propel them towards the church. The church is perceived as a steady and solid influence in their life. It may also be a place of penance. It is not uncommon for crack and ice addicts to make statements such as "I am not going to go to self-help meetings, but I am going to go straight to church and pray."

While this return to the church should be supported and reinforced as part of an aftercare or continuing care plan, the basic elements of the behavioral foundation program of recovery should never be ignored. These basic elements include self-help, physical exercise, nutrition and ongoing professional assistance. Although the church will be critical in the recovery of many crack and ice addicts, it should not be used as a replacement for self-help. In group the following statement has been heard, "The church will save your soul, but self-help will save your ass."

Traditionally, the church has been helpful to the community by allowing such groups as Alcoholics Anonymous and Cocaine Anonymous to meet within the church confines. However, the *American Heritage Dictionary* defines ministers as those who attend to the wants and needs of others. If the Gallop Poll is correct, the great wants and needs of America today have to do with the drug problem. The church should take a much stronger stance and be much more proactive in its willingness to enter as an agent of recovery. There is no doubt that a strong, united, religious, nondenominational movement could rouse a silent majority and bring the type of support needed to help those in recovery with the difficult transition back in to their communities.

It was Jessie Jackson who once said, "The drug problem will not be solved in the White House and the

State House, but in your house and my house." If the singular families in the community are influenced strongly by the church, then the church should minister to their needs. The need right now is to create tremendous support and hope through acceptance, prevention and early intervention of addictions.

Families in Community Recovery

If we consider the high-risk times of early recovery that are created by the physiological changes occurring in the body secondary to crack and ice addiction, another problem may exist in the transition back into the family. Family systems tend to have two opposing processes. One process urges the individual to make necessary changes in their life. However, the other process is diametrically opposite. This process is involved in maintaining the *status quo*, things as usual. The *status quo* has numerous triggers for relapse. Addiction must be perceived as a family systems illness. Not only a present family systems illness, but also an illness that typically involves past generations. The more dysfunctional the family, the less intellectual they will be about addictions to substances like crack and ice. They will have a tendency to be highly reactive and when the stress of an out-of-control situation, such as crack and ice addiction manifests itself, the whole family system will catalyze the anxiety.

There may be other members of the family with disorders that must be considered. These disorders may range from stress-related problems to acting out behavioral problems, all the way to addiction in other family members. One principal problem with the addict's family is sabotage. Historically, it has been very common for the spouse of an alcoholic to drink with the alcoholic to keep them company and to be a part of their life. Fortunately, it takes a period of time for most individuals to develop abusive alcohol consumption patterns. However, when the addict's significant other (boyfriend or girlfriend) uses cocaine with the cocaine addict or ice with the ice addict, a different phenomenon can be observed. Always remember that these are highly addicting, rapidly progressing drugs that establish an immediate psychological relationship with the user. Use can rapidly progress towards pure drug dependence. A clinician might hear, for example, a significant other express to treatment staff the fact that their husband or wife, boyfriend or girlfriend hit the pipe and has lost control of their crack and ice use. the crack and ice smoker then becomes the identified patient. If a thorough assessment is not performed on the significant other, often abusive histories are missed.

An assessment developed by Nuckols (1988), helps address this issue. There is a simple assessment sheet for the spouse or significant other that deals with such issues as feelings of distress, uses of cocaine with spouse and loved one, uses other drugs such as alcohol and marijuana, uses cocaine to enhance sexual relationships, enjoys the excitement of a cocaine lifestyle, and has done things to cause guilt and shame. In essence, these particular areas and others are used in this assessment to develop a picture of the significant other in regards to their use of cocaine and other drugs. This is important information because these patterns affect the addict's recovery in the community.

A woman in Cincinnati related a story about her boyfriend who hit the freebase pipe. She put him into a treatment program where he went through traditional inpatient, twenty-eight day, rehabilitation. She stated that while in the program, she went to an Alanon meeting and several educational sessions. She was, however, not asked about her use of alcohol or drugs. She stated that when her boyfriend completed treatment, she was somewhat resentful when he had to go out to many AA meetings and NA meetings. She still had her old friends and her old exciting lifestyle that was a part of the early and middle stages of cocaine dependence. She had not hit the free-base pipe, but was only a snorter and, therefore, felt that she had no problem at all with cocaine. While her husband went out to his self-help meetings, she would go out to a bar or to a friend's house to snort lines of cocaine. After her husband came home she would come home "high" on cocaine and feeling somewhat frisky. This type of behavior lead to several relapse episodes for the boyfriend.

When finally a treatment program assessed her particular use patterns, positive changes commenced for the family. She was placed into a low-intensity outpatient environment while her boyfriend continued with his continuing care program. They both went to self-help meetings and the outcome at six months was very positive with future prognosis looking very good. Her description, however, of giving up cocaine was something worthy of remembrance. She said, "A lifestyle without cocaine was like going from Rolex to Timex."

There are many other ways that significant others can cause sabotage. Many of these have to do with old dysfunctional, multigenerational dynamics often referred to as adult-children or codependency issues. The long-term recovery of the crack and ice addicted family system will depend greatly on the ability of the treatment system and the family itself to work through some of these issues that create relapse possibilities in early recovery.

There is another immediate issue, that must be looked at clinically in regard to maintaining family structure, This involves the sexual acting out that took place during the addiction. There have typically been incidents of sexual behavior that violated beliefs and values. The therapist must choose when and if these issues are to be disclosed and dealt with. A good guide for helping deal with these issues may revolve around Step Nine of Alcoholic's Anonymous. Step Nine refers to making amends for past injuries to others.

A related issue involves the anchored response between cocaine and sexual activity. Many crack and ice addicts will state that their drug of choice enhanced sexual arousal. Since scientists have found no true sex center of the brain, we can only speculate how these stimulant drugs create this perception. For one thing, crack and ice enhance feelings of positive self-esteem and self-confidence. Because of these enhancements, the risk-taking behavior may be made easier and fear of rejection reduced.

Secondly, and maybe most importantly, a drug such as crack and ice enhance sights, sounds, smells and memories associated with sexuality. Sexual arousal seems to be involved with such associations. As Nuckols (1985) states, "If cocaine can relieve feelings of performance anxiety and inadequacy, then the trap is set for the strong association between sexual behavior and cocaine. Part of the problem resides in the fact that the user attributes sexuality, sexual success, or sexual acting out, to cocaine and not to their own personality and anatomy. An anchored response between sex and the use of a drug is set into motion. This anchored response causes one to think about crack cocaine when engaged in sexual activity or to think or sexual activity when using cocaine."

Cocaine can create a false sense of intimacy when it is used as a substitute for friendship. It is the only gift that the individual who are involved in a "cocaine romance" are capable of giving to one another. Initially, the cocaine creates a way of feeling good together and it has the property of enhancing the sexual experience. However, cocaine can become necessary in a relationship that is established. This indicates something is drastically wrong. Either there is waning sex life, emotional distancing or problems with trust.

Another family related issue involves the crack or ice addict who comes from a dysfunctional immediate or extended family. Trying to get this immediate or extended family into treatment is sometimes problematic. It is found helpful to approach the family at the same time that the adolescent is admitted into treatment. If you give the family twenty-four to forty-eight hours without being involved in the treatment process, they are going to be difficult to persuade to become involved. It is also typically not useful to label the family as dysfunctional during an assessment or intake interview. The following type of statement has been found to be helpful:

"I want you to know how critical it is to your son (daughter) that you be involved in their treatment. As a matter of fact, their chances of recovery are very slim without your help. Therefore, you should start to make babysitting arrangements or to get a leave from your job so you can participate in our family weekend, family week, or family evening program."

What the therapist has done here is keep the threat of family therapy out of the initial conversation. The family hears that they are going to be needed to help someone else. In this case, the help will be focused in the direction of the identified patient or the crack or ice addict. This technique also takes advantage of the quality of guilt. For the family or significant other to say, "No, I won't come in and help out this family member," would be guilt invoking.

When the family has been through several sessions or gone to an Alanon meeting and an educational session or two, the therapist may then look at the family and state, "I bet when your son or daughter was using drugs and not showing up at home or acting out in this or that way, you felt angry (responsible, mad, frustrated)." The family or significant other then typically will respond with a verbal or nonverbal affirmation. This, in essence, has opened up the problem area from being focused exclusively on the addict to now focusing on the interplay within the family system. Now the therapist is open to looking at the family and saying, "Because you have been impacted and have gone through these feelings and these behaviors associated with addiction in the family, we have this group or this particular educational session that we are going to put you into that will help you deal with those issues."

The treatment of the family in many ways should parallel the treatment of the patient. Issues regarding the first steps as it pertains to denial, unmanageability, out-of-control behavior and looking at issues regarding changes in people, places and things will be as critical for the family as they are critical for the adolescent addict.

Family therapy for families where crack and ice addiction is present should know that the illegal nature of the drug will create some different types of problems than those seen with depressants such as alcohol. For example, the spouse of a crack addict in group once stated "Would you believe that the other night some people broke into our house, put a shotgun to my face and ripped me off for $10,000.00 and several ounces of cocaine?" When the group asked her what she did about that, she stated "I showed those sons-of-bitches, I got the best alarm system that money can buy and hooked it up directly to the police station. They will never do that again."

Obviously, this is an issue that must be confronted within the family group. However, on occasion, when there is a mixed group of alcoholics or other depressant users and stimulant addicts—especially when the depressant families have adolescent children that they suspect may be using crack or ice—a defocusing can occur. On occasion, an alcoholic family member may accuse the crack addicted or ice addicted adolescent of selling drugs to their children. Often, this is a generalized statement and not pertinent to the functioning of the group.

Crack and ice has created new dilemmas in regard to family systems treatment. We are now running into families that do not want the crack and ice addict to give up selling the drug. Dealers are very intelligent and understand that to teach the younger children and adolescents to take some of the money they earn home to mother or to the family is a good way to purchase family support. We are running into families now who have more money than they have ever had before. The financial motivation to continue to remain involved in the drug business overrides any motivation to treat the addiction.

Crack and ice addiction among adolescents has brought a new set of worries to society. That is the problem with the crack and ice babies, often born to teenage mothers. There are great numbers of such children in our communities. There is no one to love and care for them and they get minimal stimulation. In recent longitudinal studies with crack babies, it has been found that with caring and the right structure, developmental difficulties will be minimized. It may be that establishing healthy living arrangement for these children will be the difference between normal societal functioning and a tremendous handicap.

One option is to use grandmothers and grandfathers as surrogate parents for these youngsters. Certainly, there is a magic that exists between a grandmother, grandfather and grandchild. This magic can be put into socially productive surrogate situations.

A final family oriented treatment need involves the tremendous deficit in treatment facilities for young addicted mothers of small children. In regards to this population, some treatment with day care potential must be developed to meet the needs of this growing population.

Building Surrogate Families

In situations where the family is reluctant to participate in treatment or where there is behavior that is obviously destructive to the recovery of the addict, a surrogate family should be considered. The future of recovery for many adolescents will depend upon the development of living systems that allow for a positive, but yet family-like environment. The development of half-way and quarter-way houses has not yet progressed in a way that meets this need.

A *transitional living facility* can provide secondary treatment for the addicted adolescent who is new to recovery. This structured environment also gives them recovery-oriented housing with a twelve-step philosophy and solid social support for recovery. Such an arrangement could allow for some contact with family. This would especially be beneficial in regard to a family continuing therapy.

There are many models for transitional living environments. The *Carlos Institute* in St. Petersburg, Florida is one designed for those individuals who have tremendous losses and need to be taken out of their home/community environment. The *Turning Point* in Tampa, Florida is another model transitional living combined with full-time employment and a supportive community is put into play. These facilities are analogous to a "recovery motel" with live-in managers. The possibility of effective transitional programming, offered at reasonable cost, will produce higher recovery rates for youthful addicts who cannot deal with a dysfunctional family or community environment.

In sum, effective transitional living facilities need to incorporate several characteristics:

- **An emphasis on habilitation**. Because many addicted adolescents have never developed the tools needed to become competent students and workers, we need to make some provision for helping them learn these skills. To succeed, the transitional living facility must cultivate close ties to social service agencies, including those that provide vocational training, job placement, therapy, and academic alternatives such as the G.E.D.

- **A recovery "family."** The transitional living community can function as a recovery clubhouse. Here is an opportunity for the recovering young person to attend several self-help meetings each week, such as those offered by Alcoholics Anonymous, Narcotics Anonymous, and Cocaine Anonymous. The traditional emphasis these groups place on finding a sponsor for each recovering person is essential also.

Overall, the aim is for the recovering adolescent to "stick with the winners"—a group of people who model effective daily skills. This context offers the most powerful path for adolescents to learn how to make decisions, solve problems, and structure their time without resorting to drugs.

- **Direct ties to the community.** Locating transitional living facilities directly in our most distressed neighborhoods is a powerful statement of hope in itself. Through such an effort, we begin to win back our communities.

The transitional living facility provides a place where adolescents experience the basics of a healthy family: adults who set limits; people who are fair, consistent, and available. In this environment we can help addicted young people mature cognitively, emotionally, and socially. Moreover, we can offer a drug-free alternative to the kind of aversive environments discussed in part two of this book. In essence, these communities can be the fully functioning families that these adolescents never had.

. . . 7

School, Workplace & Criminal Justice System in Recovery

Cocaine, crack and ice are part of the devastating triad of school dropouts, alcohol and drug problems and difficulties with the criminal justice system.

The age of onset for introduction of crack and ice use in the high risk population is between eight and fourteen years of age. Many of these children come from dysfunctional homes where there is alcoholism or drug addiction, incest, or other forms of abuse. A child from this type of dysfunctional home—who has low self-esteem, no special skills, and low to average academic achievement—is high risk for using drugs. Crack and ice allow these individuals to cope emotionally with problems.

For many adolescents, crack and ice use is part of their culture. These children are raised in homes where drugs are used openly. Their parents are unable to deal effectively with the demands of parenting and to guide their children away from drug use.

At the other end of the spectrum, a child who is doing well in school, sports or other extracurricular activities may be able to "just say no" when a drug dealer approaches. This individual may respond with something like, "my mother would kill me" or "they will kick me off the ball team." These individuals may postpone initial experimentation with drugs until later in adolescence.

The children who start using drugs in elementary or middle school generally do poorly in school and either become truant or display behavior problem and are suspended. These students become so preoccupied with getting high they can no longer concentrate on schoolwork. As they become more dysfunctional in school they have a tendency to drop out, usually by age sixteen.

An age-related difference in addictive disease manifestation is that the process is much more rapid in adolescents than in adults. For drugs such as crack and ice, we see even a second order of problems in the progression. These two drugs tend to be much more rapid in precipitating addictive problems than marijuana or alcohol. The crack and ice use may be perceived as acting out behavior, and just a normal phase of adolescence. Some people hope that these children will just grow out of the danger. However, this is usually not true for crack and ice, where the addiction potential is so great and the progression so rapid.

In treatment programs we see young crack and ice addicts with diagnosable *Borderline Personality Disorders*. They come into the treatment programs and cannot read; they may have *Attention Deficit Hyperactivity Disorders* or *learning disabilities*. When asked to do something, they often react angrily. It is not always because they are angry about having to do a task, it is just that they do not know how, and they are embarrassed. These younger addicts tend to be high school dropouts, and many have criminal justice records. They have no vocational skills. Yet, out on the street, they can make $500 to $1,000 or more selling crack cocaine. They can have a new pair of Reeboks and a new pair of sweats every day if they so desire. They can have a gold necklace. And yet, to date, our principal intervention for this population has been "just say no."

Cocaine was once a drug for the more affluent. Amphetamine was the drug found more often in certain illegal subcultures. Now crack cocaine is readily available and packaged in unit dose costing as little as five to ten dollars per hit. This amount of money is available to most children and adolescents. Ice, on the other hand, is somewhat more expensive. It will cost more money, but because of the long duration of its effects, an adolescent can smoke it before school and the high can last all day long. For the student who wants that stimulant high, ice is much more user-friendly than crack. The high from crack is much shorter in duration and therefore it must be used more often, increasing the likelihood of getting caught.

The changes that have been made in the distribution and routes of administration of cocaine and amphetamine into the forms of crack and ice have made the drugs available to middle and lower class socioeconomic populations who previously could not afford it. Children and adolescents who previously had no exposure to crack and ice or very little exposure are now able to afford and obtain the drug.

Estroff and others (1989) conducted a study examining the cocaine abuse patterns of 479 younger adolescent patients to determine the patterns and severity of their cocaine abuse. They also examined other dimensions such as psychiatric presentation and psychobehavioral effects secondary to prolonged or increased cocaine abuse in this population.

The demographics of the sample was predominately white, with the drug abusers around sixteen years old. There were, however, fourteen-year-old cocaine addicts observed in this study. The results showed that marijuana use frequently predated cocaine abuse. The abuse of marijuana in combination with cocaine seemed to be related to the degree of cocaine use itself. Moreover, *as the cocaine addiction progressed there was a greater tendency towards the use of crack cocaine.*

The researchers also found a greater tendency towards intravenous injection as the frequency of cocaine use increased. And as the addiction progressed, so did the criminal behavior and psychological dysfunction. Selling drugs to obtain money, trading sexual favors, car theft and fighting became much more common as the use of cocaine escalated.

What the Estoff study did not look at was the correlation between crack use and school dropout. Do school dropouts have a stronger tendency toward addiction or does alcohol, crack and ice addiction precipitate school dropout? The study couldn't answer that question. All we can say for sure is that there is an association between dropping out of high school, using crack and ice, and being involved with the criminal justice system.

WHAT CAN THE SCHOOLS DO?

The school system should help the adolescent develop age-appropriate behavior. For example, from the adolescent perspective, there are developmental needs that must be met that will be important in allowing adolescents, especially in a peer context, to establish boundaries. Boundary issues involve such things as personal, social and physical status. There is also the developmental need for novelty and excitement. Adolescence is the time when a sense of self is formed, especially as it relates to peers.

Provide Support for Children from Dysfunctional Homes

Children from dysfunctional homes have special needs that must be met. Children from high-risk environments need to be taught about drugs and the dynamics of addiction. The tough question that must be asked is, if these needs are not being addressed in the family, what responsibility does the school have to the individual who spends six to seven hours per day within the system? Can our schools meet some of the needs and developmental tasks of at-risk adolescents? Can our school systems be expected to provide prevention and early interventions for these populations? Although these questions are the subject of much current debate, it is undeniable that public schools are in the best strategic position to intervene.

Our schools can and do provide drug education as early as elementary school. And drug prevention can start as early as kindergarten. Often teachers and guidance counselors identify children from alcoholic or drug-abusing homes. These children may start to show noticeable signs of problems as early as elementary school. Some elementary, middle and high schools have started "Children of Substance Abuser" groups, facilitated by a counselor from a community drug program or by the school's guidance counselor.

Create Effective Student Assistance Programs

One modality that may assist in providing positive alternatives for students with difficulties is the student assistance program (SAP). A student assistance program may recommend student assessments to help pinpoint significant changes in behavior that could suggest the early stages of a student drug problem. In this way, the student assistance program functions like a workplace employee assistance program (EAP). Assessments identify symptoms presented within the school context and seek root causes. Once root causes are identified, an accurate determination of care needs can be made.

How a student assistance program is organized seems critical to its effectiveness. Schools can move too far into diagnosis and become liable financially for the outside treatments they recommend. SAPs may recommend behavior contracts, support group participation, conferences with counselors or special education evaluation. By limiting referrals to free, community-based assessments, schools can avoid becoming diagnosticians and making explicit recommendations for admission into external clinical programs, for which they may be forced to pay.

Schools can provide positive alternatives for students who have been suspended for alcohol or drug use. One alternative is to arrange for the student and parent(s) to attend drug education classes. Another is for the student to have a drug assessment provided by a local drug treatment center, usually free of charge. If the student is willing to seek help, then a shorter suspension might be negotiated.

There is a need for good communication between the juvenile justice system and the schools concerning the adolescent who is on probation and ordered by the court to attend school. The student and the student's probation officer need to have a contact person in the school. This contact person could be from the student assistance program, or someone whom the principal designates. A student on probation should be able to have regular meetings with this contact person to help with any school problem. Also, the student's probation officer could have regular meetings to track the student's progress.

Create School-Based Programs for At-Risk Students

Another strategy is to establish a school-based program for students in need of substance abuse or family counseling. These programs are designed to assist adolescents who need alcohol and drug treatment, while remaining in their school environment. These programs typically help the adolescent eliminate or reduce alcohol and drug use, improve school attendance, improve academic achievement, demonstrate positive classroom behaviors, learn healthy alternatives to drug use, develop a healthy self-image and improve family relationships. One such program is the *New Horizons Program*, developed by the Center for Drug-Free Living in Orlando, Florida in cooperation with the Orange County School System. This program was started in the high schools in 1977 and the program was expanded into the middle schools in 1987 in response to this population's need for such services.

Students involved in New Horizons are identified in several ways. Administrations and police-liaison officers refer students who have been caught possessing or under the influence of alcohol or drugs in school. Teachers who suspect students of abusing drugs and alcohol—based upon frequent absences, declining grades, drug talk and mood swings—refer them to the New Horizons counselors. Guidance counselors refer students who are drug users or those having a family problem involving alcoholism or drug use.

One barometer of the program's success is that many students request help for themselves or their friends when made aware that this kind of counseling is available on the school campus. The New Horizons counselors work closely with the school attendance personnel in identifying students considered high-risk for dropping out due to personal or family involvement in alcohol or drug use.

Upon referral, the New Horizons Counselor interviews the student and makes an assessment. This assessment determines the degree of treatment necessary. If the student agrees to participate in the program, the counselor completes an evaluation, which include a drug, psycho-social and school performance history. The students who are admitted into the program receive individual, group and family counseling focusing on the drug and school attendance problems.

This program uses trained therapists with master's degrees in the behavioral sciences. The counselors are at the school Monday through Friday. They have daily groups with the identified drug-using students and also groups for the children of alcoholics and drug users. Their work is geared towards helping students meet socialization and other developmental needs related to their use of alcohol and drugs or helping them cope with addiction in their family. An interesting aspect of this program is that it carries elective credit; the students attending this program receive credit as they would for any math or history class.

In an effectiveness study of the program, 93 high school clients and 79 middle school clients were evaluated. These were students admitted to New Horizons from August 1990 through February 1991 and who had participated in the program through the end of the school year. It was believed that students admitted in March, April, or May had not been in treatment long enough for us to evaluate our effectiveness with them. Other students treated this year—who were not included in the study— were those who withdrew from our program before the end of the year. In almost all of these cases, the student either dropped out of school or was referred to another treatment program. A few were incarcerated, and a few others were discharged for noncompliance with program rules.

Two school-related measures of effectiveness were evaluated: (1) grades; and (2) attendance. The grade-point average (GPA) from the first nine weeks was compared with the GPA from the fourth nine weeks of school for most students in the study. For students who entered the program in the second semester (from late January on) we used the GPA from the second nine weeks compared with the GPA from the fourth nine weeks. This was an attempt to use the GPA closest to the time of admission.

We found that for the *high school* students in the New Horizons program:

- Forty-six percent improved their grade point average;
- Forty-eight percent either maintained a C or better average or improved their starting grades to at least a C average;
- Fifty-five percent improved either their grades *or* attendance;
- Sixty percent completed the program successfully and ten percent were referred to other treatment programs.

We found that for the *middle school* students in the New Horizons program:

- Forty-four percent improved their grade point average;
- Fifty-three percent either maintained a C or better average or improved their starting grades to at least a C average;

- Fifty-three percent improved either their grades *or* attendance;
- Seventy-seven percent completed the program successfully and six percent were referred to other treatment programs.

Some of the student participating in the New Horizons program are recovering. These are students who are reentering school after inpatient treatment. These adolescents need this kind of continuing support and counseling to remain drug-free.

The New Horizons programs concluded that reduced school dropout rate was an element associated with the reduction in alcohol and drug use. This is an extremely important criteria when viewing the potential productivity of a population of people who tended to have a higher dropout rate.

Still another approach has been described by the Youth Guidance Center in Rhode Island (Wingo, 1988). The intent of their *East Bay Substance Abuse Prevention Program* is to conduct school-based intervention for students who are identified as high-risk individuals. The focus of this particular program is on the development of: (1) skills to resist substance use and abuse; (2) problem-solving skills in an attempt to enhance coping skills; and, (3) social competence. The program strengthens the child's ability to cope with the stressors and demands faced in everyday life. The skills developed within this project will enable these children to cope more effectively on a social level and make more responsible decisions regarding their life. The specific target of this program was the preadolescent, based on the 1985 study that indicated that on the average, children first drank alcohol in the ninth grade and that some 100,000 children ages ten to eleven reported getting drunk once a week. The goal of the East Bay Substance Abuse Prevention Program is early intervention, with a prevention initiative.

Crack and ice are readily available and marketed to a younger and younger population. It is not uncommon to see eight- and nine-year-old stimulant addicts in treatment. The school system could be a recovery resource not only through their kindergarten through sixth grade prevention efforts, but through ongoing assessments and in-school intervention. The student assistance programs, school-based treatment programming, as well as the prevention programming described above represent a start in establishing a cooperative relationship between communities and their schools. They also demonstrate the symbiotic relationship between community-based programming, treatment programming, the school system and the criminal justice system. It is only be through a concerted effort that society will see a reduction in the number of addicted adolescents.

THE WORKPLACE

There are shadow industries competing with American industry, not for marketshare or customers but for the minds and souls of our consumers. The product sold by drug cartels and drug gangs—cocaine in its various forms—is four to seventeen times more valuable than gold, the often-used universal standard of value. This makes these new commodities, crack and ice, precious and, to many, desirable. They are easily marketed to adolescents and to young adults entering the workforce. This means big trouble for American companies.

The Threat

It is only when we look at crack and ice as commodities that we understand how the principles of supply and demand energize this shadow industry. As long as the mass media makes pronouncements like, "Ice hits faster and causes a greater euphoria than crack cocaine," there will be tremendous advance marketing for the drug. As long as we are a nation cut off from our spiritual roots, a drug that is marketed as potent and euphoria-producing, will be held in high esteem.

It appears that there will be a strong demand for stimulant drugs during the decade of the nineties, as adolescent addicts move through the school system and into the workforce. What about the issue of supply? In regard to cocaine and especially crack cocaine, it is currently a buyer's market. The quality of the drug is high and the quantity may even exceed the demand. In the early 1990's, there were some isolated reports of incredibly large busts. Tons of cocaine have been apprehended in single seizures. A tunnel from Mexico into Arizona was discovered. However, criminal justice and the treatment system do not report reductions in the number of crack addicts entering jails and treatment centers.

For the drug dealer, crack cocaine is the perfect marketable substance. It is product that causes a consumer to enter an immediate love affair with it. Therefore, it creates a high incidence of repeat consumers. It is a high mark-up drug with incredible profit margins. It also follows the basic marketing principals of the pharmaceutical industry. Instead of having to buy a large amount, an individual can buy a very small amount—a *unit dose*. This allowed for more people to have access to the drug at what appears to be a lower price. The marketing of crack cocaine created the current scenario for the introduction of a similar drug, ice.

Adolescence is a time when many enter the workforce. It is certain that the combination of stimulant and other drugs in the workplace will create grave dangers to health, productivity, safety, product quality, health-care costs and morale.

The pressure that drugs bring to bear on the workplace is extreme. Chronically addicted adolescents form a significant portion of the labor pool from which businesses in the 1990's will draw workers. Never before has the concept of early intervention and prevention made so much sense. The prognosis for corporations with crack and ice addicts will depend largely on the ability of the corporation to respond quickly and effectively before the valuable employee becomes a late, middle or chronic stage crack or ice addict.

What Can Corporate America Do?

There are many approaches that must be consistently taken, and supported by top-level management, that are crucial in helping to reduce the trend of drug use in the American business environment.

Prevention goes hand-in-hand with early intervention. All employees should be educated regarding the signs and symptoms of drug abuse. This is not only crucial for the supervisor and line employee, but it extends all the way into the functioning of the employee's family. If corporate America creates a "family culture," then it must address the problems of the extended family or the significant others involved in employee problems. This is crucial economically because an addicted employee will probably have a three hundred percent increase in health benefits and other benefits claimed by the family.

All key personnel should have advanced training in the signs, symptoms, and assessment of addiction. These key personnel include upper level management, supervisors, individuals working in risk management, the medical department, and especially the employee assistance professionalss. They should be given clear-cut and simple guidelines for what to do with an employee who is perceived to be experiencing a drug problem. These key people are not doctors and cannot diagnose. They must, as any other good manager would do, identify signs and symptoms of job performance decline. This decline in performance will be the lever that can be used in any form of intervention with the employee.

Those responsible for referring a troubled employee into an environment for professional assistance need to know more than just signs and symptoms. They need to understand the basics of treatment as well as how to choose a good treatment program. For example, an employee assistance professional needs to be able to ask questions of a treatment facility such as:

- What types of programming do you have for addicts?
- Do you see any difference between the treatment of crack and ice addicts and a depressant addict?
- Where does relapse occur and what are you doing to prevent such relapse?
- How is the jobsite incorporated into treatment?
- Does your continuing care plan involve a return-to-work plan?
- How is the family integrated into treatment?
- Is the significant other assessed adequately for their own use of substances such as crack and ice?

- What are you doing to promote recovery within the jobsite, community, and school.

These and other questions will help those professionals who are involved in the assessment and referral of addicted employees make the best and most enlightened choice.

Addicts Do Not Recover in Isolation

Addicts must have support. Putting an addict back on the same shift or even changing shift, puts him or her into constant contact with others who are using drugs. Therefore, it is important to create a "culture of recovery" within the workplace. The addict should report to the employee assistance professional or other designated individual daily for the first few months into recovery. There should be a "buddy system" in place. Another cooperating worker can be assigned as a buddy to the newly reintegrating employee. This individual can help the newly recovering addict structuring their time at the worksite.

A newly recovering addict must change old patterns involving people, places and things. It will be the initial task of the treatment program working cooperatively with the employee assistance professional or other job professional, in conjunction with the buddy system, that allows for the changing of "playmates" and "playpens" on the jobsite.

An important part of a recovery culture involves self-help. Many industries today offer self-help meetings at the worksite. A lunchtime, dinnertime or other break-time access to self-help meetings is crucial to promoting socialization with other recovering individuals.

The transition back into the workplace after treatment is very intimidating for addicts. They will have to deal with such issues as money owed to them or money owed to someone else. They are expected to explain to fellow employees and to their drug-using friends what has gone on during their absence. In order to support the individual through this rough period, there must be an active recovery culture within the organization.

Interpersonal environmental elements are principal determinants of relapse. If recovering employees are not supported in their reentry into the workplace, they will have a tendency to behave the same way they did while addicted. This keeps them with the people, places and things associated with their earlier drug use, especially if they were heavy users at the worksite.

Employee assistance professionals and other key individuals should be actively involved in the employee's treatment. They should visit the treatment facility and communicate with the addict. There should be at least one return-to-work session that spells out clearly the expectations of the employee assistance professional and the employer. It is sometimes productive to have the employee return to the worksite for this session. In this way, key personnel can be involved in the planning session and the addicted employee can put a foot back onto the worksoil before formally returning to work. This eases feelings of anxiety and defines clearly what is expected.

A return-to-work plan should be created by the employee assistance professional and the addicted individual. This return-to-work plan can be a part of the continuing care or aftercare plan, or it can stand alone. It should be signed by both the EAP or company representative, or other company representative, and the patient. Although it is not legally binding, this is a clear written agreement spelling out the behaviors necessary to enhance the possibility of recovery. One copy of this contract should be put with the employee's patient chart, another given to the employee, and the original copy kept by the employee assistance representative.

Issues to be covered in this contract include an authorization for a company representative to consult with the treatment team during continuing-care therapy. A commitment to work a Twelve-Step program on and off the job would be stated within this contract, along with an agreement to participate in the company's buddy system, if one exists. How frequently the employee will meet with the EAP representative during a period of time should be spelled out precisely. There should be a clause stating what actions will result from failing to keep a certain number of consecutive appointments.

It is highly recommended that addicts agree to a plan to identify and control personal cues or anchors in the workplace that could lead to a relapse. The addict should describe, sometime during treatment, how they will manage each of these internal or external relapse cues. This return-to-work plan should articulate what the addict will do if severe drug cravings are experienced at work.

The plan should be so detailed as to include: (1) where the recovering addict should park; (2) how they should take their breaks; (3) with whom they should have lunch; and, (4) give permission for the returning crack and ice addict to use whatever services are available within the company to assist them in their recovery. Remember that therapeutic permission must be consciously and explicitly given. It is not enough just to say, "I am available." It must be spelled out to the returning-to-work addict that the employee assistance professional, for example, is available at any time during the workday to meet with them.

We recognize that the approach described above is very comprehensive and time-consuming. With drugs such as crack and ice—where the craving is so severe and relapse so impulsive—attention to detail is crucial. When we realize that *treatment is preparation, but recovery involves successful transition and reintegration*, then detailed and explicit return-to-work planning makes sense. The key to responding successfully to the threat of addiction in the workplace involves creating a healthy oppositional sub-culture to drugs, a counterforce, a culture of recovery. This culture of recovery includes providing the means for initiating the earliest possible intervention when drug abuse is detected. It mandates the cooperation of treatment professionals and workplace professionals as it pertains to reintegrating the addict into the workplace.

THE CRIMINAL JUSTICE SYSTEM

Addicted adolescents and young adults are entering the criminal justice system at an alarming rate. The federal government's "zero tolerance" stance has not worked. There has been little deterrence resulting from this policy. Our courts, juvenile detention centers and prisons are overcrowded. As addicts take up more of the space available in our prisons, more violent offenders are sometimes released early.

The relationship between criminal justice and treatment has been controversial and sometimes competitive. When a synergistic relationship exists between these two systems, results are positive. A model for such synergy can be found in the TRACK 5 program offered by PRIDE, Inc. of West Palm Beach, Florida.

TRACK 5 is a comprehensive and innovative program for the treatment of addiction. Its target population includes the criminal justice client whose behavior and recidivism indicates a chemical abuse problem. The typical TRACK 5 client is facing significant incarceration as a result of violating probation or multiple drug arrests. These clients are older adolescents and young adults, typically with nonviolent histories.

In general, incarceration is neither cost-effective nor significantly rehabilitative for this population. Unfortunately, effective and affordable treatment has not been available for this group of individuals, especially those who abuse *crack*. Residential treatment, when available, is extremely disruptive to the individual's life, very expensive, and rarely long enough to treat the addiction effectively.

Using an outpatient model, TRACK 5 allows clients to learn recovery skills while gaining employment. For many, this may be the first time they have been gainfully employed. The duration of treatment, twelve months, is sufficient to allow recovery skills to solidify and supports the client through the extensive process of recovery. Active treatment is then continued in an aftercare program that supports clients for as long as they choose. The *alumni network* involves successful "graduates" in various programs and allows them to share their success and strength with new referrals.

Because addiction—especially in the 1990's—is a multidimensional problem, a program must seek to treat all the areas of *life health*. Programs that focus primarily on drug use are almost always ineffective because they ignore other vital areas of necessary rehabilitation in the client's life. In TRACK 5, clients are assessed and provided treatment in all areas of life: social/family health, physical health, occupational/vocational health, emotional health, and drinking/drug-use health. Research indicates a model that ignores deficits in any of these areas is much less likely to facilitate long-term, meaningful recovery.

In order to understand the TRACK 5 concept, it is important to see the separate components that make up the program. Through the complex relationship of all these interventions the quality and effectiveness of the program has been exceptionally high. Some of the most important components are described below.

Case Coordination

Each client has, from the time of admission, a case coordinator. This individual is a trained specialist in the treatment of addiction and will follow a client's progress for the duration of the program. The case coordinator is the conduit for all information. Face-to-face sessions, minimally once a month, monitor and assess client progress in all areas of the program. The presence of this professional facilitates change, maximizes progress, and notes problems in recovery before they reach a crisis stage. In client evaluations, this individual is rated the most important feature of the program.

Group Therapy

Research indicates that group therapy is the most effective type of therapy for working with addicts; moreover, it is the most cost-effective. Clients spend two evenings weekly with their small core group working with a trained group therapist. They will spend the entire twelve months with this group and therapist, creating a level of group dynamics seldom achieved in a traditional outpatient model.

Family Program

Family participation has long been recognized as essential to a client's recovery. However, in a world of nontraditional families and complex social interactions its focus has been too limited. The Family Program brings the significant persons in a client's life into a therapeutic support group. Participants are involved in three separate support and education groups, including the therapy group. By treating the significant others, as well as the client, the complex social interactions are repaired and refocused.

Employment and Vocational Assistance

The TRACK 5 program maintains a unique relationship with the Private Industry Council. Clients who are assessed to require employment and vocational assistance are referred directly to the Private Industry Council for services. The client is maintained in active treatment, which significantly improves the likelihood of success in Private Industry Council programs. Their individual treatment plans, through both agencies, are reciprocal and interrelated. Through open dialogue, both problems and progress are noted and reinforced between agencies.

Basic Education

Clients in an addiction treatment program often have a history of poor educational participation and often lack a high school diploma. Even clients with a diploma lack basic mastery in many skills. TRACK 5 maintains a liaison relationship with the Palm Beach County School Board to refer clients for services, generally to classes to provide preparation for G.E.D. testing as well as to refine and improve basic skills.

Recreational Programs

Many clients active in addiction treatment have lost the ability to structure leisure time effectively. Too often, their leisure time was spend in drug-related activities, either obtaining or using drugs. Recreational therapy seeks to teach basic leisure skills and involves them in a variety of positive pursuits.

Educational Groups

This twice-weekly group incorporates the educational portion of the program. Topics related to dependency and recovery are addressed and reinforced. Awareness and understanding of the development and features of addiction is essential to long-term recovery. Also, this forum allows for presentation of a variety of information related to healthy lifestyle development and maintenance. The educational component of the TRACK 5 program is unique in that it follows no preset format or topic schedule. Client participation is mandatory.

Specialized Optional Services

Numerous referral services complete the TRACK 5 program. Individual, couples and family therapy are available within the program. Acupuncture treatment is available at a reduced fee upon client request. Spiritual counseling also is available on referral. TRACK 5 maintains a strong liaison relationship with area residential treatment facilities for clients who require brief, inpatient treatment as part of the program. Comprehensive treatment is the primary goal of TRACK 5.

Self-Help Groups

Clients are introduced to the various Twelve-Step programs in the area and will develop strong ties with these organizations as part of the program. The TRACK 5 program recognizes the importance of the Twelve-Step recovery community as a vital component of a client's long-term recovery, especially upon completion of primary TRACK 5 treatment. All TRACK 5 clients have an identified "Sponsor" and "Home Group" as an intermediate treatment goal.

Aftercare Group

Clients enter a specialized Aftercare Program during the last two months of Track 5. This program is designed to facilitate maintenance of learned recovery skills in the community as the client completes active TRACK 5 treatment. Clients may continue with Aftercare at their discretion beyond a two-month minimum requirement.

... 8

Success is Possible

Guiding chronically addicted adolescents to a lifetime of sobriety is a task of frightening complexity. The odds against their recovery can seem so overwhelming, and our resources so few, that we can legitimately wonder if we're equal to the task.

At these times it helps us remember that addiction treatment isn't rocket science. Our approach to addicted adolescents is far more art than science. Empirical research in the field can give us some overall perspectives. But our day-to-day interactions with these young people can be as profitably guided by another directive: Do what works. And if it's not working, then change something.

Common sense and doing what works are wonderful concepts that psychology sometimes ignores. Those of us who are treatment professionals can become frustrated, especially if we were trained in many different disciplines, to discover that many of the technique we were trained to use come to naught. It's important to realize that mere technique, even when paired with a sophisticated under-standing of psychological theory, can actually make us less therapeutic.

Consider, too, what we ask of the addicted adolescents who enter our lives. It's been said that recovery from alcohol and other drug addiction amounts to a simple task: *Just change everything, and do it now.* We can bring this saying to mind whenever we want to remind ourselves of the long road we ask these young people to travel.

Remember also that drug use is one of the many expedient, if highly flawed, tools these adolescents used to survive. Rather than asking them to instantly abandon their worldviews, we can instead ask for simple changes in behavior. Indeed, treatment for any kind of addiction keeps returning to the same task: making simple changes in the people, places, and things formerly associated with drug use.

Possibly the greatest contribution to be made by community-based recovery is that this approach is subject to few constraints by therapeutic teachings and traditions. In building ties to the community, as suggested in this book, we can experiment radically and settle on approaches that suit each individual. The process is utilitarian, guided by ideas such as "keep it simple," "stick with the winners," and "do what works."

The greatest gift we can give—parent, teacher, or professional—is to be fair, consistent, and available. Much of what we've written in this book is simply a footnote to this fundamental idea.

Finally, we can be walking proof that there are satisfying alternatives to addiction. It is in sharing our experience, strength, hope that we can light the path of recovery for an addicted adolescent. My interview with Sharon Dyson, a counselor, shows how this happens.

The Interview

Paint for me a picture of a memorable client—anyone who comes to mind.

One of the clients who comes to my mind a lot is Martin. He was from a lower-class family in a migrant town. Mom had him when she was fourteen years old. Martin never knew who dad was.

Martin's mother later married when she was seventeen years old and had three other children. His stepfather did not want Martin to come over and see mom or visit any of his stepbrothers and stepsisters. So Martin grew up with his grandparents, who were growing and picking oranges all their lives. He got everything he wanted because they felt so sorry for him.

When he came to MACO, Martin had three charges of possession of cocaine. I would say he was not learning disabled but he was in that program because of his environment. Still, he had very good diction for his type of environment. Lack of social skills was, more than anything else, his problem.

Martin was real special to me because I knew that this kid had it. No one ever gave it to him; no one just put him on a level where he should be. Because I wanted to give him so much, I could identify what he had going for him. I started out working with him, working with some reading skills—not really doing an assessment on him but just getting him in a place where he felt free to read and speak with the other clients here.

He was very bashful. Martin was taught never to say anything unless someone spoke to him or asked a direct question. And as far as him talking about his feelings and his parents and about his grandparents . . . well, usually in the black culture it is a 'no-no' to talk about anything that happens in the house. So he wouldn't give any information about what happened at home. He wouldn't tell me about any of this feelings; he wouldn't open up to any of the rest of the clients, and he was just real tight in a shell. He knew he needed to do all these things but just didn't know how to do them.

It got to a point where I would see Martin maybe twice a day for the two-week period he was here. He was just a real special person because he began to open up. He began to show me that he did have good reading skills and good learning skills. He told me everything I wanted to know about the family. It ended up where I was picking him up on Saturdays and finding him a job.

What were all the specific areas you were working on with Martin throughout the day's sessions? You talked about socialization skills and vocational rehabilitation. Explain the deficits you felt he had to overcome to mature to a productive individual.

I think the main thing that he had that was not recognized was his social skills. We had to pull things out of him at first. But after talking with him about communication skills and getting along with other folks and letting people know what your feelings are, I think the ideas stayed with him: 'It is okay that I am feeling this way; if I am not feeling happy or if I am feeling sad or if I am feeling confused, that's okay, too. I can let people around me know how I am doing and what I am feeling.' It also felt good for him to talk about the family, which was always a secret.

When he finally did start letting things out about the family, it was a real good thing. But there were also some sad things. He didn't have anyone to talk to. Plus he was living with older people who had a 'hush-hush, no-no' attitude toward problems. For Martin, it was this: 'I am into my own world, and that is why I am selling drugs—because I know that I have to survive for myself.' So I would say working with feelings was Martin's biggest thing.

You are talking a lot about grief issues. For example, what sorts of things caused him to go inside of himself?

Family issues.

Any in particular?

The lack of love from his stepfather. Martin got a lot of love from his grandparents, but it wasn't the kind of love that he was seeing other children getting from their parents. No parental love was the problem, I would say.

Martin felt singled out, neglected.

Yes. And I think this is harder with adolescent boys than it is with girls. The girls have the frilly bows and hairdos when they are little, and when they are big many of those things are still okay. But guys have to change in a different way. They're supposed to be masculine at a certain time, and they have to go into different peer groups. They have to decide who they want to be, and that is real difficult for them.

Martin was caught up in one of those gray areas. He more or less he presented himself in a decent way; he dressed in a decent way; he had good skills, good diction skills, good communication skills. But he just didn't know what to do with all of it.

Do you know what happened to him when he left?

Yes. Martin is doing great. He is in a New Horizons program and is the senior person running it right now. He is also a manager at Taco Bell, his first job. He is participating in a lot of church activities. His community service is done, and he's been taken off of probation. He's also attending South Eastern Counseling and is one of the oldest people still attending there. He completed the program and is still going for continuing care.

That is an amazing success story. It's far different than the typical story: the adolescent goes back into his family environment and gets back into the same behavior. They go back into a situation where there is a lack of structure and consequently find it hard to sustain the changes they began in treatment. You talked about a couple of things that were important in helping Martin avoid that scenario. One was keeping him in school and the other was getting him into a program at school that seemed to help him. Will you tell me about that program and why you chose it?

It's a drug prevention program called New Horizons. Usually it's an elective program, so the kids choose whether to take it or not. Martin was more or less forced into it because he was dealing drugs. Martins friends in the course were a different type of crowd than the people he usually hung out with. Even his drug-involved peers thought New Horizons was a cool thing to do then. It's like: 'Wow, are you going to get into Horizons course? That's real neat.'

If I were to go into the New Horizons program, what would I get out of it? What would they teach me?

You'd get education about the different drugs and their effects.

Would they monitor my use or would they work with me in any other way?

I think they would monitor your use, but it is more of an education and prevention program.

You also talked about getting Martin involved in the church. How did you work the church into his treatment plan?

I'll tell you, this goes back a lot further. Martin and I are from the same town, so I figured that was the perfect thing for me to do was take him to my church and get him in the youth program. After I talked with his grandma, she decided that she wanted to join our church, too. So their family came with my husband and me, and they joined the church. Martin got active in Usher Board and the Baptist Youth Fellowship. With my husband and I participating, he just kind of followed through. We have about maybe 175 youth in our church. I think the youth make the church.

You are a teacher of the church?

Yes, exactly.

I think there is an important point here. Most of the time there are turf issues that limit what a therapist will do out in a community and how involved the therapist will get with a client in a community. Often clear-cut lines are drawn: You do not socialize with your clients; you don't see this person out in the community; you have nothing to do with them.

Most of those lines have been drawn based on incidents of inappropriate socialization, sexual contact, and exploitation. But it seems to me that treatment now has to be community-based. And to be effective, therapists have to know the strengths of the community and use those strengths to get the individual involved.

I definitely agree.

I have just been impressed with that about you, with your willingness to go beyond what happens in the treatment center and stay involved out there. Do you think you can work without that level of involvement?

I really don't—not in my community. I'll say something for black folks, something that's only my belief: I think we need total involvement, because trust is so hard. It takes a lot more for a black child or even an adult to give someone that complete trust. And that is why I feel I have to give to someone else, because I want that trust.

To me, you have to be in the community. We have to take folks from the community and then work within the community to integrate them back in to the community. It's also important to take kids out of the community and provide them with a healthy environment *before* you put them back in. Kids want the cohesiveness constantly. They need to be able to come knock on my door and say, 'I was here two years ago and I still need to talk with you.' And I need to do something besides say, 'Well, we finished our deal last year, so you are done. I got new folks here.'

We have these programs for kids, and yes, you have to be productive. But there is not a point where I say to an adolescent: I am done with you. That happens so much. I see the kids come in for a two-week assessment, and they've never had any type of treatment. They don't even know what we are doing, and then, boom, they are out of here. They don't have anything to hold onto.

So I say this to the kids: 'If I take an assessment and you don't need any treatment, let's still do something. Let's still have a little contact. If you are going to out-patient treatment, residential treatment, whatever, just give me a call and let me know how you are doing.' I still want that little piece to hold on to. Maybe I am wrong, because I can't save the world. But it makes me feel good to know that you are doing something about yourself, that you got your beginning. Your roots are formed. This makes me feel good, and I want more.

Another thing is important, especially in a low income communities: Often there's a real continuity in those neighborhoods. People stay there forever. If there is a church, they all attend the same church for thirty years. If there is a store, they go to that same store for thirty years. If I am giving you support, you are going to send your kids to me and get the same support.

I think that the work you do is an exercise in delayed gratification!

Oh, definitely.

It is marvelous to get those calls back from former clients. And you really have built other families for these kids. You have created a whole community-based surrogate family for them through the church, through the school system, through the relationship with you, and through the relationship with another outpatient therapist. That's what really seems to be working now. Now for another question: Are you running into a lot of problems with gangs?

No. But I run into a lot of kids who are selling more than using.

How do you deal with that?

I ask these kids, 'What are your accomplishments? How far do you think you will get as a dealer? And when you get caught, what's going to happen? What are you going to do, and how much money do you think you can make?' Then I ask them, 'What if your sister was doing drugs, and what if your mother got on them?' That usually brings them down a little bit. These kids really don't have the education they need about drugs. They don't really know what a drug is.

Let me ask you one final question, an open-ended one: Suppose you were making a list of things you would like to have available for your clients. There are no monetary constraints or system constraints; you could just build any program that you wanted. What would the components be?

One would have to do with education. Another is to fill the need within the black community for more black counselors. Often they can more easily understand what these kids are going through. Sometimes when white counselors come into the drug field they assume the children they see are on drugs. Many times black children are more into making money than being on drugs; even so, these children are often told they're in denial about drug use. It is real hard to understand how black kids can want to make money before they use. Another important thing is helping the kids talk about what is going on with them and at home.

It makes great sense to me. You're seeing that the problems are so much greater than alcoholism and drug addiction.

References

Chapter Two

Grinspoon, L. and J. Bakalar. 1976. *Cocaine: A drug and its social evolution*. New York: Basic Books, 17.

Lerner, Michael A. 1989. The fire of ice. *Newsweek*, November 27: 37-40.

Siegel, R. 1987. Cocaine smoking disorders: Diagnosis and treatment. *Psychiatric Annals*. 14(10): 730-35.

Gold, Mark. 1984. *800-Cocaine*. New York: Bantam Books.

Chapter Five

Shapiro, D. 1989. *Psychotherapy of neurotic character*. New York: Basic Books, 9.

Millman, R. 1986. Considerations on the psychotherapy of the substance abuser. *Journal of Substance Abuse Treatment* 3: 103.

Brothers, L. 1989. Empathy: Therapeutic and biological views. *Harvard Medical School Mental Health Letter*. 6(5): 4-6.

Chapter Six

VanDusen, W. and Sherman, S. 1974. Cultural therapy - a new conception of treatment. *Journal of Psychedelic Drugs*. 6(2): 174.

Alcoholics Anonymous. 1953. *Twelve steps and twelve traditions*. New York: A.A. World Services, 44.

Brown, S. and Yalom, J. 1977. Interactional group therapy with alcoholics. *Quarterly Journal on the Studies of Alcohol*. 38: 426-456.

Flores, P. 1988. *Group psychotherapy with addicted populations*. New York: Haworth Press, 125.

Wallace, J. 1989. Ideology, belief and behavior. In *Writings*, J. Wallace. Newport, RI: Edgehill Publications, 338.

Apthorp, S. 1988. Drug abuse and the church: Are the blind leading the blind? *The Christian Century*. Nov 9: 101-103.

Cairns, T. 1990. Beginning a ministry with substance abusers. *Home Mission Board*. Southern Baptist Council.

Nuckols, C. 1988. *Schedule C: A clinical self-assessment.* Bradenton, Fl: Human Services Institute.

Nuckols, C. 1985. Cocaine, intimacy and sexuality. *Focus on the Family*. November-December, 16.

Chapter Seven

Estroff, T., Schwartz, R. and Hoffman, N. 1989. Adolescent cocaine abuse. *Clinical Pediatrics*. 28(12), 550-55.

Wingo, D. 1988. Program provides training to socially inept at-risk youngsters. *The Addiction Letter*. 4(11).